COMPUTER APPLICATIONS IN FIRE PROTECTION ENGINEERING

Edited by
Paul R. DeCicco, P.E.

Volume III
Applied Fire Science in Transition Series
Paul R. DeCicco: Series Editor

BAYWOOD PUBLISHING COMPANY, INC.
Amityville, New York

Library of Congress Catalog Number: 00-041430
ISBN: 0-89503-224-4 (Paper)

Library of Congress Cataloging-in-Publication Data

Computer applications in fire protection engineering / edited by Paul R. DeCicco.
    p. cm. - - (Applied fire science in transition series ; v. 3)
  Includes bibliographical references and index.
  ISBN 0-89503-224-4 (paper)
    1. Fire protection engineering- -Data processing. 2. Fire protection
engineering- -Automation. I. DeCicco, Paul R., 1924- II. Series.

TH9210.C65 2000
628.9'22- -dc21   00-041430

Contents

INTRODUCTION

Computer Applications in Fire Protection Engineering

Since the use of computers in almost every domain of fire safety has become so universal over the past decade, it might seem a difficult exercise to select material to feature in a volume with the above title. However, there are two areas in the use of computers which merit special attention because of their profound effects on design and analysis processes relating to almost every aspect of fire safety in general and fire protection engineering in particular.

The area of computer use of most universal interest is that of fire modeling. Computer-based models are now used in the development of almost all fire safety plans for major buildings and structures. Computer-driven mathematical models are used to examine and predict consequences that may result from various imposed fire scenarios and they are part of most post-fire investigations of origin and cause.

The second domain of computer utilization which is of growing interest is the incorporation of decision-making processes which use expert system intelligence. In these endeavors, the model makes choices about alternative options as it seeks solutions to problems involving optimum exiting design, issues relating to human behavior, and consequences to the overall outcome of the fire which might result from failure of elements of building and/or fire protection systems. Given the ubiquitous role of computers in fire protection engineering, there also arises a need for critical review of the many programs coming into use including consideration of their reliability and limits.

In this volume, Sullivan, Terro, and Morris present a *Critical Review of Fire-Dedicated Thermal and Structural Computer Programs*. In this chapter, seven different thermal analysis programs and fourteen structural models are examined. The authors discuss the theoretical background to the programs together with their strengths and weaknesses. Some comparative benchmark testing was also carried out.

Beard, in his chapter *Reliability and Computer Models,* discusses sources of error in the process of using a model and offers a general categorization intended to help stimulate discussion and further work. These categories include: Unreality of the theoretical and numerical assumptions in the model; the numerical solution

1

techniques; software error; hardware faults and application of the software by a particular user. He concludes that fire models should only be used in a supportive role and results need to be interpreted in the light of limitations of the model and other knowledge and experience.

Donegan and Taylor describe two prototype expert system applications to assist in the evaluation of dwelling fire safety. The first based on the philosophy of point schemes where knowledge is elicited from expert opinion. In the second, the rules are formulated on the basis of published guidelines. The former displays a "what if" potential for active/passive trade-off between different measures of fire safety. The latter offers an advice domain.

In their chapter, *A Model of Instability and Flashover*, Beard, Drysdale, Holborn, and Bishop present a non-linear model FLASHOVER A1, within a zonal formulation which may be used to predict the geometrical and thermo-physical conditions which lead to an instability in the system. The existence of a critical fire radius is demonstrated at which the state becomes unstable. The authors suggest that it would be desirable to attempt to insure that the fire radius remains below the critical value. The importance of flashover in the course of a fire and heretofore difficulties in predicting its occurrence make this offering of value both in the design of measures to prevent it, and in the consideration of risks to firefighters who need some way to anticipate the phenomenon.

Casciati and Faravelli discuss *Causal Probabilistic Networks with Learning* as a diagnostic decision tool. The chapter provides a framework in which the operative conditions of existing buildings can be assessed on a probabilistic basis. The decision maker system is able to learn from the expertise it collects during its service. The supporting mathematical tool makes use of a causal probabilistic network to represent the knowledge domain. The authors give an example of the process.

In *Limitations of Fire Models,* Beard discusses the limitations of computer-based fire models in general terms. Zone models and CFD-based models are considered. The author suggests that numbers assigned to parameters for use in models give rise to uncertainties with numerical input associated with physical parameters; numerical solution techniques; software error; hardware faults and application error. He concludes that a model examination group for assessing fire models is needed and cites studies which have been made of four models including: ASET, HAZARD_I, FIRST and JASMINE (1.2), and the work of the Fire Models Context Group sponsored by the Home Office in the United Kingdom.

Jia, Galea, and Patel describe *The Numerical Simulation of Fire Spread Within a Compartment Using an Integrated Gas and Solid Phase Combustion Model.* The integrated model includes several sub-models representing different phenomena of gaseous and solid combustion. The authors use the integrated model to simulate a fire spread experiment conducted in a half-scale test compartment and discuss the areas of agreement and disagreement between results of the simulation and the actual fire experiment.

In *Numerical Modeling of Radiative Heat Transfer in Integrated CFD Fire Modeling,* Keramida, Souris, Boudouvis, and Markatos, set out to provide fire modelers with guidance on the engineering treatment of radiation transfer. Two widely used radiation models are reviewed and their performance is assessed in a benchmark experimental enclosure fire. The discrete transfer and six-flux radiation models are compared in terms of computational efficiency, ease of application, and predictive accuracy. The authors conclude the effect of thermal radiation is important, even in small fires and that the simple six-flux model suffices for small compartment fires up to 100 kW.

CHAPTER 1

Critical Review of Fire-Dedicated Thermal and Structural Computer Programs

P. J. E. Sullivan, M. J. Terro,
and W. A. Morris

This chapter presents a survey of available numerical methods used in the thermal and structural analysis of buildings in fire. The problem of structural response of buildings to fire is normally broken down into two distinct parts. First, a thermal analysis is performed which considers heat transfer to and heat flow within the building elements. This is followed by a determination of the mechanical response of the heated elements and their interaction with the rest of the building. In the work described in this chapter no less than seven different thermal analysis programs and fourteen structural analysis models have been identified [1]. All of these programs are in common use and can be employed to provide data as supporting evidence for regulatory compliance. Little work has been previously presented by way of general validation for these methods. More commonly, programs are validated against specific and limited test data. In achieving a good correlation between theory and practice it has been observed that it is necessary to make a number of assumptions, often in an arbitrary and empirical manner. This often means that the accuracy of output is determined by a pre-knowledge of the result. Such methods have to be used with caution and understanding. The work described in this chapter discusses the theoretical background to the programs together with their strengths and weaknesses. Some comparative bench mark testing was also carried out.

Traditional structural design methods include large safety factors, thus reducing the risk in fire. Currently, building codes of practice implement the concept of limit state of failure in design, which although more economical to implement, does not operate under the same levels of safety factors. The use of limit state

5

methods should, therefore, be investigated to cover the design of buildings under expected hazardous conditions such as fire. The current process of design for fire is based on testing and prescriptive techniques with pseudo engineering methods for interpolation and extrapolation. Other areas of engineering do not use such out-of-date methods of design. Instead, rational procedures have been adopted based on probabilistic and deterministic calculations [2].

The current Building Regulations permit structural fire calculations and states that:

> The building shall be so constructed that, in the event of fire, its stability will be maintained for a reasonable period

The key word in this clause is "building," yet, current methods of testing only consider single elements. The stability of buildings during a fire can only be practically assessed using numerical methods.

The Approved Document B2/3/4 "Fire Spread" of the Department of the Environment [3], in support of the Building Regulations, recognizes that a satisfactory performance of a complete building structure is difficult to determine with the current state of fire engineering analysis. In view of this difficulty, it is suggested in the document that an acceptable solution can be achieved by considering results from tests on single elements providing good design practice with respect to other loads at ambient temperatures is followed. The problem of analyzing complete building structures under fire can be effectively addressed using numerical engineering methods.

Numerical methods have been applied to structural analysis since the 1960s, but computer programs dedicated to the analysis of buildings exposed to fire did not appear until a decade later. Most of the currently available programs have grown out of a number of research projects within universities or research establishments. Consequently, the programs tend to be badly structured, because the aim of the researcher is to further the science rather than to produce commercial software. A badly structured program is also inevitable as the researcher tries out various options, and then discards many of them as the work proceeds, but the discarded options often remain in the source code. A corollary of the badly structured program is poor documentation. In contrast, the large commercial software packages are well supported and documented, but the numerical models available tend to lag behind those used for research purposes. In general, the developers of the commercial software packages have not produced efficient fire temperature material models.

Commercial software packages required in the past large mainframe computers and could not be operated within the PC environment. However, with the rapid increase in computer power and technology this limitation is being overcome and many designers and product developers look toward computer modeling as an economic supplementary method to furnace testing, as a means of performance verification. The ever increasing costs of furnace tests is contrasted to the falling costs of computer software and hardware. The time scale associated with the setting up and executing of fire tests can also be significantly greater than the time required to run a computer analysis of the same problem. Additionally, numerical analysis offers greater flexibility in the choice of geometries, sizes, materials and boundary conditions.

The development of analytical techniques in structural fire engineering have been very slow, but the general level of awareness in the area of numerical modeling is growing and it is only a matter of time before these methods will be widely used by the industry.

The object of the work described in this chapter is to provide a critical review of, and recommendations on, no less than twenty one existing computer programs and their theoretical background.

Nearly fifty research workers in the field were contacted world-wide as follows:

1. Personal contact followed in some cases by meetings.
2. A detailed questionnaire was sent requesting specific information on the theoretical background of the methods adopted in modeling the effect of fire on the structure.
3. Benchmark tests were sent to authors and users of programs to solve specific thermal/structural problems.

Nineteen organizations responded positively to the contacts, and the result was that seven thermal analysis programs and fourteen different structural analysis programs have been included in this study. All of these programs are in common use and their authors claim that they can be employed to provide data as supporting evidence for regulatory compliance.

The descriptions provided in this work are based on the information received from the authors who were sent drafts for approval. In some other cases, very limited information was released by the authors, presumably because of commercial confidentiality. It was, therefore, not possible to include a description of such programs.

The numerical modeling of the effect of fire on the structural behavior of buildings has been the subject of considerable research in recent years. The majority of this research work has been concentrated in universities and other research institutions. Professional software companies, such as LUSAS, ADINA and ABAQUS, have recently started to have some interest in this field.

A survey of currently available fire-dedicated thermal and structural analysis programs is presented in this chapter. The information in this survey is based on available literature and private communication with the authors of the programs described and of necessity is dependent on the details provided.

This survey was only concerned with fire-dedicated computer models where it was possible to contact the authors of the programs during the time devoted to complete this work. Bench mark exercises were conducted with the assistance of the authors of programs covered in this survey. A summary of the conducted survey on thermal and structural programs is presented in Figures 1 and 2, respectively.

THERMAL ANALYSIS PROGRAMS

The number of existing software capable of analyzing the thermal response of materials under transient heating conditions is quite large since heat flow analysis is used in many engineering disciplines such as aeronautics, mechanics, electronics, electrical, etc. Some of these programs were developed in professional software houses, such as LUSAS, ADINA, ABAQUS, etc. These programs have many advantages including documentation, sophisticated nonlinear material models, pre/post-processing facilities, etc. The others were developed by academic research institutions and by private consultancies, such as MANIFOLD which is owned by ETA Engineering Consultants Ltd.

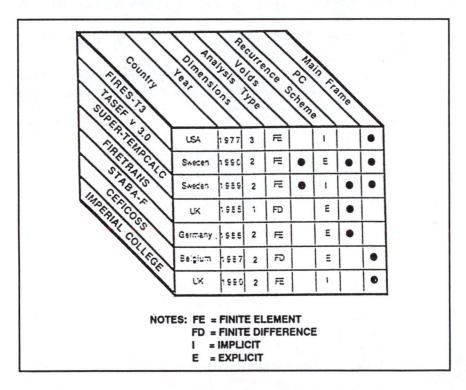

Figure 1. Summary of survey on available fire-dedicated thermal analysis computer programs.

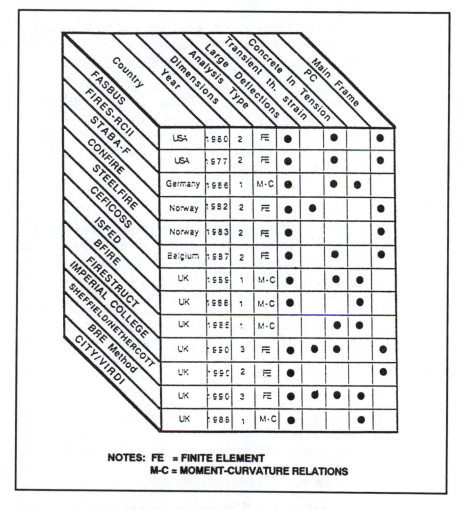

Figure 2. Summary of survey on available fire-dedicated
Structural analysis computer programs.

The following assumptions have been taken in the thermal analysis programs discussed in this chapter:

- The fire exposed material is assumed to be homogeneous, and effective values of thermal properties are used in the input data.
- The full effects of moisture movement and pore pressure build-up, including spalling are neglected in all programs.

- The calculation of the radiation and convection fluxes at the boundaries is simplified by the use of a resultant emissivity and convection factor which are derived by comparing predicted and measured temperature data in furnace tests.

However, despite the above-mentioned simplifications, complete reliance cannot be given to measured temperature data because of its dependency on the test conditions. Therefore, predicted temperatures using thermal analysis programs may be, in some cases, more reliable than the measured data. A few well-known fire-dedicated programs will be briefly described.

FIRES-T3

FIRES-T3 (FIre REsponse of Structures-Thermal, 3 dimensional version), is a nonlinear finite element thermal analysis program designed for the prediction of the temperature history in three dimensional continua exposed to fire conditions [4]. FIRES-T3, which can model the thermal flow in three dimensional continua, was developed by R. Iding, B. Bresler, and Z. Nizamuddin at UCB in 1977. This development research work was sponsored by the National Science Foundation and the National Bureau of Standards.

FIRES-T3 is capable of predicting the temperature distribution history in one, two or three dimensional continua consisting of different materials under fire attack.

The finite element library consists of:

1. Eight noded hexahedron and six noded tetrahedral isoparametric elements for three dimensional analysis.
2. Four noded quadrilateral and three noded triangular isoparametric elements for two dimensional analysis.
3. Two noded isoparametric bar element for one dimensional analysis.

The boundary conditions in FIRES-T3 can be Prescribed heat flow at the boundaries, known temperatures at nodes, or convection and radiation at the boundaries. FIRES-T3 can also analyze the exothermal heat generation of the body as a function of volume and time.

Heat transfer due to convection and radiation at the boundaries can be linear or nonlinear where the heat transfer coefficient is input as a function of temperature.

The thermal conductivity, specific heat capacity and density of the material are allowed to vary with temperature. The surface and gas properties are kept constant during the thermal analysis. The authors of the program recommend the use of a resultant emissivity ranging between 0.5 and 0.7 for concrete structures exposed to fire.

The time integration solution procedure implemented in FIRES-T3 is the backward difference implicit scheme.

TASEF

TASEF (Temperature Analysis of Structures Exposed to Fire), is a nonlinear finite element thermal analysis program devoted to the prediction of the temperature distribution history in two dimensional structural sections due to fire attack [5,6]. TASEF was first developed as a part of a PhD research work by U. Wickstrom of the National Testing and Research Institute (SP) in Sweden. The latest version of the program, TASEF v 3.0, was developed in September 1988 [7].

TASEF is capable of describing the thermal response of two dimensional continua consisting of different materials exposed to fire. The structural section may include internal voids where the heat transfer by convection and radiation are taken into account. The heat transfer by radiation across an internal void is modeled by considering the view factors of the surrounding surfaces.

The TASEF software package consists of two major routines: INTASEF and TASEF. INTASEF is the input data generator for TASEF. INTASEF is a very simple interactive pre-processor, as described by the author of the program.

The finite element library in TASEF consists of four noded rectangular and three noded triangular elements.

The thermal conductivity is allowed to vary with temperature in TASEF. The heat capacity is indirectly input by giving the variation of the specific volumetric enthalpy with temperature. The specific volumetric enthalpy is used to take into account the latent heat effect due to evaporation or to chemical reactions taking place at high temperatures.

TASEF can model heat flow problems with internal heat generation, specified heat flux at the boundaries, known temperatures at nodal points, or convective and radiative boundary conditions. The convective flow at the boundaries can be linear or nonlinear.

The convection factor, convection power, and resultant emissivity are assumed to be independent of temperature. The developers of TASEF recommend the use of the following values for the surface parameters when analyzing structures exposed to test furnace conditions (these values may vary with furnaces):

ε = 0.6 and 0.8 for steel and concrete surfaces respectively.

β(W/m K)   = 2.2 and 1.0 at the unexposed surface and the fire exposed surface in a model fire test respectively, and twenty-five in the case of an exposed surface in a furnace test.

γ = 1.25 and 1.33 at the unexposed surface and the fire exposed surface in a model fire test situation respectively, and unity in the case of an exposed surface in a furnace test.

The time integration solution procedure employed in TASEF is the forward difference (explicit) scheme. To avoid stability problems that could arise in an explicit scheme, TASEF calculates the critical time increment at every time-step as a function of the material thermal properties and mesh size and varies the size of the time-step accordingly. The critical time increment is the time-step limit above which instability problems in the solution occur.

SUPER-TEMPCALC

SUPER-TEMPCALC is a finite element thermal analysis program [8] devoted to the analysis of two dimensional structural sections exposed to fire boundary conditions. SUPER-TEMPCALC was developed by Fire Safety Design (FSD) consultants under the supervision of Y. Anderberg in Sweden in 1989. The program is a further development of TEMPCALC which was released in 1985 [9, 10].

SUPER-TEMPCALC is capable of predicting the temperature history in structural sections consisting of different materials exposed to fire. Internal voids in a section are modeled by considering the energy consumed in heating the air.

SUPER-TEMPCALC is linked to graphical pre- and post-processors and a material database. The pre-processor produces the finite element mesh automatically and extracts the thermal properties from the material database. The post-processor presents the results on the screen and on a plotter with temperature contours at different times.

The finite element library in SUPER-TEMPCALC consists of four noded rectangular and three noded triangular elements. The coordinates of nodes can be given in cartesian or cylindrical reference systems for use in axi-symmetric elements.

There are three types of boundary conditions in SUPER-TEMPCALC:

1. Prescribed temperatures at nodal points at the boundary.
2. Radiation and convection boundary condition.
3. Boundary with the temperature of the gas taken as the average of surrounding nodes, i.e., internal voids.

The thermal conductivity and the thermal heat capacity are allowed to vary with temperature.

The resultant emissivity and convection factor are allowed to vary with time in SUPER-TEMPCALC. Anderberg recommends the use of a resultant emissivity value of 0.5 and a convection factor of 25 W/m K. The recurrence scheme employed in SUPER-TEMPCALC is claimed to be unconditionally stable, i.e. independent of the size of the time-step.

FIRETRANS

FIRETRANS is a one dimensional finite difference thermal analysis program [11] developed to predict the transient temperature distribution through a composite slab subject to fire attack at its soffit. This program was developed by Ove Arup & Partners (OAP) under contract to the Building Research Establishment (BRE). The program was completed in June 1985.

FIRETRANS is capable of predicting the temperature history distribution in a composite slab exposed to fire at the bottom face and cooling to ambient air at the top surface. FIRETRANS can only perform one dimensional heat flow analysis and is based on the finite difference theory of heat transfer.

The output data from FIRETRANS is interfaced with the structural analysis program FIRESTRUCT developed by OAP. The temperature calculations are carried out in a first step prior to the structural analysis calculations.

Up to seven layers with different materials properties can be specified in FIRETRANS. However, in the finite difference equation each layer is automatically divided into four and temperature is calculated at the interface of these sub-layers. The thermal conductivity and the thermal specific heat are allowed to vary bi-linearly in FIRETRANS. The density of the material is assumed to be constant.

At the hot surface, the flame temperature is specified at uniform time intervals in the input data. At the cold surface the room temperature is assumed to be constant. The heat flow at the boundaries is derived using linear convection at the cold face and radiation and convection at the hot face.

A constant value of film conductance, H in W/m C (equivalent to convection factor) is employed. H can vary from 0 for a perfectly insulated surface to 10^{99} for a surface without thermal resistance.

The time integration method used in the heat balance equations in FIRETRANS is the forward difference (explicit) scheme. This scheme necessitates the use of small time-steps for the stability of the results. The input time-step is automatically checked in FIRETRANS against a calculated critical time-step value. If the time-step is not found adequate, the program rejects it and asks for a new value.

STABA-F

STABA-F is a nonlinear thermal and structural analysis program [12, 13] devoted to the study of uni-axial structures under fire attack. STABA-F was developed at the Institut für Baustoffe, Massivbau und Brandschutz of the Technical University of Braunschweig in West Germany.

The thermal analysis in STABA-F is achieved using a finite element method coupled with a time-stepping scheme. The thermal properties are nonlinearly temperature-dependent. The surface heat transfer parameters are kept constant during the analysis.

The finite element library consists of three noded triangular and four noded rectangular elements. The integration time-steps employed in STABA-F has to be chosen small enough to assure convergence and stability of the analysis. A time-step range between 2.5 and five minutes with a rectangular network having a maximum width of 20 mm is recommended by the developers of the program.

Since out-of-plane deformation is taken into account in STABA-F, there is no reason why fire problems with asymmetric heating of the cross section cannot be modeled. Further, since the sizes of the time-step and the element mesh are restricted for convergence, STABA-F appears to be based on the explicit recurrence scheme.

CEFICOSS

CEFICOSS (Computer Engineering of FIre resistance of COmposite and Steel Structures), is a nonlinear two-dimensional finite element/finite difference program designed for the thermal and structural modeling of steel and composite steel-concrete structure in fire [14]. CEFICOSS was initially developed by J. M. Franssen as a PhD research study at the university of Liège, Belgium. This research work was sponsored by ARBED, a structural steel manufacturers' company, in Luxembourg under the supervision of J. B. Schleich and was completed in November 1987.

The calculation of the temperature distribution in CEFICOSS is achieved using a finite difference approach and it is only capable of solving two-dimensional problems with one axis of symmetry orthogonal to the heating direction. A rectangular mesh is used to discretize the cross section of the structural member. The same rectangular mesh is employed in the through thickness integration of the member in the structural analysis. The time-stepping integration algorithm employed in CEFICOSS is the forward difference Euler (explicit) scheme. The size of the time-step is varied during the calculations to ensure convergence.

The thermal module in CEFICOSS can solve problems with ISO 834 temperature-time relationship or any other type of fire exposure at the boundaries. The resultant emissivity, convection factor and power are kept constant whereas the conductivity and volumetric heat capacity are allowed to vary with temperature.

A simplistic moisture migration model is implemented in the thermal module in CEFICOSS. In this model, the free water residing in an element is allowed to evaporate at 100 C and then move to a cooler neighboring element where it condenses. This model does not take into account a number of factors affecting moisture movement including the porosity of concrete, preferential routes for moisture movements, effect of cracking, etc.

Imperial College/Thermal

A nonlinear finite element heat transfer analysis designed for the prediction of the temperature distribution history in two-dimensional continua was developed at the Imperial College of Science, Medicine and Technology [15]. This program was developed by the first author, M. J. Terro, as part of a Ph D project under the supervision of P. J. E. Sullivan and G. A. Khoury. The program was completed in March 1990 on the VAX 8600 mainframe computer and is now being implemented on a PC at FRS.

The Imperial College program is capable of describing the thermal response of two-dimensional continua consisting of different materials exposed to thermal loading at the boundaries.

The finite element library consists of four-noded general quadrilateral isoparametric elements and three-noded triangular elements.

The general finite element equation is implemented in an incremental formulation to account for material nonlinearities. The residual of the heat balance equation is checked for convergence against a user-defined value. The number of limiting iterations that can be carried out until convergence at any time increment is also defined by the user in order to optimize computer time.

The thermal properties allowed to vary as functions of the average temperature of a finite element are listed below:

- The thermal conductivity k.
- The volumetric heat capacity $C \times \rho$.
- The convection factor β.
- The convection power γ.
- The resultant emissivity ε.

The heat flow at a boundary exposed to convection and radiation can be either described by giving a tabular set of time-temperature values or it can be automatically calculated in the program to model the BS 476 furnace heating.

A number of points at which the temperature history is required can be specified in the input data file. An automatic search and two-dimensional interpolation is then carried out and an additional output data file containing the temperature history of these points is created. This facility was initially developed to read the temperature value at pre-defined Gauss points for the structural analysis program.

The Imperial College program employs a Backward difference time integration algorithm. This integration scheme is implicit and has no limitation on the size of the time-step for stability and convergence.

STRUCTURAL ANALYSIS PROGRAMS

Despite increasing interest in the field of structural fire protection, the number of available programs devoted to the structural analysis of buildings under fire is limited. The majority of these programs were developed as research projects and most of them are limited in their application. Therefore, considerable research work is still required to bring the state of knowledge in the field of numerical modeling of structures under fire to an acceptable and reliable level.

Available mechanical material properties data at high temperatures needed in the constitutive models of structural analysis programs is also limited and requires further research work. For example, the structural response of a member under fire is very sensitive to the stress-strain relation at high temperatures on which available measured data is still incomplete in certain areas (e.g., concrete data in tension).

The following assumptions have been commonly adopted in the structural analysis programs presented:

1. Plane sections remain plane (Navier-Bernouilli hypothesis).
2. Perfect bond between steel and concrete, i.e., slip between the two materials does not occur in programs modeling reinforced concrete and composite steel-concrete structures.
3. Torsional effects are ignored.
4. Moisture effects are not considered.

FASBUS-II

FASBUS (Fire Analysis of Steel BUilding Systems), is a nonlinear finite element structural analysis program designed for the numerical prediction of the response of two-dimensional steel structures in fire [16]. FASBUS was originally developed as a research project at the Illinois Institute of Technology under the supervision of R. L. Chiapetta. This research project started in 1968 and resumed in 1972.

FASBUS is capable of modeling of the time-history structural behavior of two-dimensional floor systems subject to thermal loading. In FASBUS, the simulation of the restraining effects produced by framing elements (e.g., columns, beams, etc.) is achieved by adding to the input data file stiffness over and above the global stiffness matrix at the corresponding locations. However, FASBUS does not take account of three-dimensional effect of end restraints on a slab.

The finite element discretization in FASBUS is achieved by using two noded beam elements and three noded plate bending elements. The through thickness integration is achieved by layering the cross section of both types of elements horizontally. Up to eleven layers or Gauss points are allowed through the thickness. The finite element mesh in FASBUS is limited to a maximum of seventy-five elements and 180 nodes.

The temperature distribution analysis is carried out using FIRES-T3 [4]. The completed temperature file is interpolated to obtain temperature at the Gauss points of the layered structural elements.

Geometric and material nonlinear effects are taken into account in FASBUS. FASBUS can model the effect of forces in the three global directions, and in-plane bending moments about x and y axes. However, out-of-plane bending is not allowed in the beam elements. The external loads are applied at the nodal points of the structure. Furthermore, uniformly distributed loads can be applied over the surface of the plate elements. The boundary conditions can be free, simple, pinned or fixed.

FIRES-RCII

FIRES-RCII (FIre REsponse of Structures-Reinforced Concrete frames), is a nonlinear finite element structural analysis program designed for the numerical prediction of the behavior of two-dimensional framed reinforced concrete structures exposed to fire [17]. FIRES-RC, an earlier version of FIRES-RCII, was first developed by J. Becker and B. Bresler as a research project at the University of California, Berkeley (UCB) in the United States in 1974 [18]. This research work was sponsored by the National Science Foundation. FIRES-RC was revised and an updated version of the program called FIRES-RCII was developed by R. Iding, B. Bresler, and Z. Nizamuddin at UCB in 1977. This research work was sponsored by the National Science Foundation and the National Bureau of Standards.

FIRES-RCII is capable of predicting the response of reinforced concrete frames to particular loading and thermal histories. The structural solution procedure in FIRES-RCII employs a two-dimensional two-noded beam element to discretize a structure. The beam element has six degrees of freedom: Two translations and one rotation at each node. Geometric and material nonlinear effects are taken into account in FIRES-RCII. The temperature distribution history in a cross section is produced using FIRES-T [19]. The finite element mesh adopted in the thermal analysis is used in the through thickness integration of the structural analysis of the member under study. FIRES-RCII runs in a mainframe environment.

STABA-F

STABA-F is a nonlinear thermal and structural analysis program devoted to the study of uni-axial structures under fire attack [12,13]. STABA-F was developed at the Institut für Baustoffe, Massivbau und Brandschutz of the Technical University of Braunschweig in West Germany.

STABA-F is a combined nonlinear finite element and analytical solver computer program devoted to the prediction of the behavior of uni-axial members of structures under fire. The temperature analysis is performed using a nonlinear finite element routine. The structural calculation routine is based on a simplified nonlinear moment/curvature calculation algorithm at elevated temperatures. STABA-F is capable of modeling the effect of fire on: Structural steel, reinforced concrete, and composite concrete-steel members. Geometrical nonlinear interaction between load and deflection, P-d effect, is taken into account.

The computer program consists of three calculation stages:

1. The temperature distribution history across the section of the uni-axial member.
2. The determination of the nonlinear interaction between bending moment and curvature at a given temperature distribution.

3. The calculation of the bending moment, shear force, slope of the member, and deflection in accordance with the second order theory of structural analysis.

The stiffness of the structural member is updated as a function of the degradation of the material properties at high temperatures in STABA-F. This iteration, which uses a Newton-Raphson technique, results in a quick convergence in most problems. The support conditions can be simple or continuous.

The material properties are stored in material data base files which are interfaced with STABA-F. Currently, these data base files include siliceous aggregate concretes, rolled steel, hot formed steel and prestressing steel.

CONFIRE

CONFIRE is a nonlinear structural analysis finite element computer program devoted to the study of the response of reinforced concrete plane frames in fire [20]. CONFIRE was developed by N. E. Forsen during his doctorate work at the Norwegian Institute of Technology in 1982.

CONFIRE is capable of modeling the response of two dimensional reinforced and prestressed concrete structures made of quartzite aggregates in fire. The finite element discretization of the structure is achieved using a three noded beam element with ten through thickness Gauss-Legendre integration points.

The temperature data required for the structural analysis in CONFIRE is produced using TASEF-2 [6]. However, a different thermal analysis program called TEMPCALC was used at FRS to provide the necessary data by interfacing the temperature output file with CONFIRE.

CONFIRE runs in a mainframe environment using a VAX 8600 computer machine running under VMS operating system. CONFIRE is also available on a ND 5000 computer under SINTRAN operating system from Norsk Data.

STEELFIRE

STEELFIRE is a nonlinear structural analysis finite element computer program devoted to the study of the response of plane structural steel frames in fire [21]. STEELFIRE was developed by N. E. Forsen for MULTICONSULT consultants in Norway in 1983. The programming language in STEELFIRE is FORTRAN 77.

STEELFIRE is capable of modeling the structural response of two dimensional steel frames subjected to in-plane loading at high temperatures. Like CONFIRE, STEELFIRE is based on a program called "CONFRAME" [22] and developed by E. Aldstedt at the Norwegian Institute of Technology in 1975. Out-of-plane deflections are not taken into account. Geometric and material nonlinear effects are considered in STEELFIRE.

The thermal analysis necessary for the fire analysis is achieved using TASEF-2 (a thermal analysis program developed by U. Wickstrom in Sweden).

CEFICOSS

CEFICOSS (Computer Engineering of the FIre resistance of COmposite and Steel Structures), is a nonlinear two-dimensional finite element/finite difference program designed for the thermal and structural modeling of steel and composite steel-concrete structures in fire [14]. CEFICOSS was initially developed by J. M. Franssen as a PhD research study at the university of Liège, Belgium. This research work was sponsored by ARBED (a structural steel manufacturers' company) in Luxembourg under the supervision of J. B. Schleich and was completed in November 1987.

The computer analysis in CEFICOSS is subdivided into three parts:

1. Linear analysis of the structure at ambient temperature conditions.
2. Temperature analysis.
3. Nonlinear analysis of the structure at elevated temperatures.

The linear structural analysis at ambient temperatures is carried out to obtain the initial state of displacement prior to fire. During the course of the program steps 2 and 3 are repeated in an interactive manner until collapse. However, the influence of the structural response on the thermal properties is not taken into account.

The structural finite element solution in CEFICOSS employs a two-noded two-dimensional beam element with three degrees of freedom at each node: two translations and one rotation. The temperature distribution is calculated using a finite difference approach with one axis of symmetry in the heating conditions. The support conditions can be free or fixed with any degree of freedom. It is also possible to include hinges between elements. Nonlinear geometric and material effects are taken into account.

CEFICOSS can be either run in a PC or a mainframe environment using the VAX or FPS computers. The hardware and software requirements for running CEFICOSS in a PC environment include an OS/2 operating system, six MB of RAM, and sixty MB of hard disk space.

Graphical pre- and post-processing facilities exist in CEFICOSS which were described as "rather use-friendly" by Franssen. Currently, CEFICOSS is being used commercially at ARBED in Luxembourg and as a research numerical tool at the university of Liège in Belgium. CEFICOSS is not supported in the United Kingdom.

ISFED

ISFED (Integrated Structural Fire Engineering Design), is a nonlinear structural analysis computer program designed for the prediction of the fire response of simple members of structures [23, 24]. ISFED was developed by Kevin Towler under Fire Safety Design consultants (FSD) as part of a contract with the Fire Research Station (FRS). The development of ISFED was completed in March

1989. ISFED was written in a PC environment using the QuickBasic programming language.

ISFED is capable of analyzing the structural response of simple one dimensional building members under fire attack. The program was originally developed with the intention of checking the validity of the different available constitutive models used for predicting the behavior of materials when heated. Consequently, ISFED is not capable of analyzing complicated structural forms.

The temperature input data for ISFED is produced by interfacing with a suitable temperature analysis program. Currently, the temperature history data input is provided by TEMPCALC [9, 10]. A rectangular finite element mesh has to be used in both the thermal analysis and the through thickness integration in ISFED. ISFED includes an option that enables the user to analyze half of the section in cases of symmetric heating regimes.

A graphical display post-processor is integrated within ISFED. This post-processing facility can be used to monitor the gradual thermal and mechanical changes in the cross section of the member exposed to fire.

A structural member in ISFED is represented by a single beam element having two supports at its ends. Different temperature profiles along the beam can be analyzed. The support conditions can be simple, axially restrained, or fixed against rotations at both ends of the beam. A combination of support condition types however, is not possible.

The material data is given to the program in a database style. Currently, the material database in ISFED includes gravel concrete, lightweight concrete, and steel.

BFIRE

BFIRE is a nonlinear structural analysis program designed for the analysis of simple building members in fire [25]. BFIRE was originally written by G. Newman of the Steel Construction Institute (SCI) in 1988. Later development work on the program was carried out by G. Newman and K. F. Chung at SCI. BFIRE runs in a PC environment.

BFIRE is capable of analyzing simple members of structures exposed to fire attack. Flexural and axially located members of structures can be studied using BFIRE. The support conditions can be simple, pinned, fixed, or partially restrained.

The temperature data necessary for the fire analysis, which is usually based on experimentally measured data, has to be manually input into BFIRE.

FIRESTRUCT

FIRESTRUCT is a computer program devoted to the prediction of the behavior of large panel systems in fire [11]. This program was developed by Ove Arup & Partners (OAP) under contract to the Building Research Establishment (BRE).

FIRESTRUCT is capable of predicting the deformation history of individual panel systems under uni-axial loading conditions in fire. The boundary conditions can only be isostatic, i.e., simply supported or pin ended.

Geometric nonlinear effects are not included in FIRESTRUCT, i.e., small displacements and small strains are assumed in the theory of the program. Therefore, the P-δ effect is ignored.

The derivation of the temperature profile during fire is achieved using FIRETRANS [11].

Imperial College/Structural-LUSAS

LUSAS (London University Stress Analysis System) is a general purpose finite element software package designed for the analysis of general engineering problems [26-29]. LUSAS was originally developed at Imperial College in the mid 70s by P. Lyons who founded FEA (Finite Element Analysis) in the United Kingdom in 1981. LUSAS has been recently developed to include the effect of fire on three-dimensional building structures as part of a PhD project by M. J. Terro under the supervision of P. J. E. Sullivan and G. A. Khoury at the Imperial College of Technology, Science and Medicine [15].

The Imperial College program is capable of predicting the structural behavior of general three-dimensional building structures in fire. The program can model reinforced concrete, steel, and composite concrete-steel structures exposed to high thermal loading. This includes columns, beams, one-way and two-way spanning slabs, slabs connected with beams and columns, etc. However, the validity of the model has only been checked against reliable furnace test results on simple reinforced concrete members which were available.

The thermal analysis is preformed separately as a first step using a nonlinear finite element program developed by the first author, M. J. Terro [15]. The integration points for the structural analysis are pre-defined by the user and input in the thermal analysis program. An automatic search and two-dimensional interpolation is then carried out in the thermal analysis program and a corresponding temperature file is created and interfaced automatically with the structural analysis program.

A pre- and post-processor module called MYSTRO is linked to LUSAS [28]. The pre-processor in MYSTRO allows the user to input data in an interactive and user-friendly fashion, whereas the post-processor permits the plotting of various illustrative diagrams including the geometry of the structure in its deformed and undeformed shapes, the time-deflection curve, stress contours, etc.

Sheffield University/Nethercot

A finite element program has been developed at the University of Sheffield for the analysis of the behavior of steel frames in fire conditions. The development of the program was started by Sharples (MPhil thesis completed in 1987) and extended as a PhD research project by Hassan Saab (PhD thesis completed in 1990) under the supervision of D. A. Nethercot [30].

This program is capable of modeling the behavior of two-dimensional steel frames exposed to thermal loading. It permits the calculation of the critical temperature and the collapse load of a structural steel component and provides a load-deformation and the temperature-deformation history for two-dimensional multi-storey steel frames.

The effect of temperature variation along and across a steel member can be considered. The temperature data is based on measured results in fire tests. Variation of temperature across the width of an element is not taken into account. Consequently, asymmetric heating, which would require a three-dimensional approach for calculating the out-of-plane bending effects, cannot be modeled using this program.

BRE Method

A non-linear structural analysis finite element program has been developed by Yong Wang at the Building Research Establishment (BRE) in 1990 [31]. The development of this program was started at BRE in 1989 with the intention of producing an alternative to ISFED using a finite element approach.

The BRE program is a finite element software capable of modeling the defor-mational behavior of three-dimensional reinforced concrete and steel struc-tures under fire attack. Although the program is capable of modeling the three-dimensional behavior of structures including torsion, it has only been validated by test data carried out on two-dimensional members.

The temperature history data necessary for the structural calculations at high temperatures can be provided to the program using two alternative methods:

1. Input and output data from TEMPCALC. The input data from TEMPCALC is used to describe the rectangular mesh across the section of a member of structure.
2. Measured data at certain locations across the section. This data would have to be input manually and a two-dimensional interpolation routine automat-ically calculates the temperature value at various points of the cross section.

Temperature is assumed to vary linearly along the length of a member of structure.

ABAQUS

ABAQUS is a general purpose nonlinear finite element software package devoted for the analysis of general engineering problems. ABAQUS was origin-ally developed by Hibbit, Karlsson and Sorensson Inc. (NK & S) in the United States in 1970. Development work on the program is ongoing.

ABAQUS is not devoted to the fire analysis of structures. However, it includes thermal and structural analyses modules in addition to a range of nonlinear material constitutive models at ambient temperatures including steel and concrete. ABAQUS runs on a mainframe computer.

Structural Dynamics Research Corporation (SDRC), based at Herts are the agents of ABAQUS in the United Kingdom. ABAQUS is used extensively by UKAEA Technology on a consultancy basis.

ABAQUS is capable of performing one, two and three dimensional thermal and structural analyses of building structures at ambient and high temperatures. The pre- and post-processing facilities in ABAQUS are very good.

City University/Virdi

A nonlinear structural analysis program called SOSMEF (Strength Of Steel Members Exposed to Fire) devoted to the analysis of simple steel members under fire has been developed at the City University in London [32, 33]. SOSMEF is still under development as a PhD project (to be submitted in 1992) by N. Jeyarupalingam under the supervision of K. S. Virdi.

SOSMEF is capable of predicting the behavior of simple structural steel beams and columns subjected to three-dimensional loading under fire. A concrete model has been recently included in SOSMEF. This would allow the program to deal with concrete and composite steel-concrete members. The support conditions can be simple, pinned, fixed, or partially restrained.

Currently, the temperature input data necessary for the structural calculations is obtained by using the thermal analysis program TASEF-2. Alternatively, experimentally measured temperature data can be input into SOSMEF.

CONCLUSIONS AND RECOMMENDATIONS

As can be seen in Figures 1 and 2, no less than fourteen different structural analysis and seven thermal analysis programs have been identified. All of these programs are in common use and can be employed to provide data as supporting evidence for regulatory compliance.

This work identified difficulties in making comparisons because information on programs and assumptions were hard to obtain.

Numerous computational methods exist which are now being used widely. None of these methods are completely satisfactory as the expertise is often "author-specific." This is a "black box" approach where results have to be accepted in good faith. A solution to this problem is to develop sound "theoretically open" programs.

Thermal Analysis

1. On the whole the thermal programs were capable of predicting temperature distribution in heated structures despite some of the simplifications adopted (see below).
2. In some cases experimental temperature measurements were in error (due for example to excessive moisture movement around the thermocouple tips) and consequently the computer predicted temperature regimes appeared to be more reliable than experimental data.
3. Thermal computer programs normally use boundary condition parameters (such as resultant emissivity) derived empirically. The values of these parameters are often "adjusted arbitrarily" without appropriate scientific explanation to make the computer predictions fit experimental results.
4. Errors between prediction and experiment normally found at temperatures of about 100–200°C for concrete structures subjected to fire are due to the fact that none of the programs consider fully and adequately moisture migration within the structure.

Structural Analysis

1. Unlike thermal programs, structural programs have not on the whole adequately predicted structural behavior, although the predictive capability of the programs varied considerably. In some cases, a second structural analysis was undertaken using the same program but with a pre-knowledge of the results so as to arrive at "improved" predictions.
2. The reasons for poor predictability can be attributed to:
   - *Inadequate input of material properties.*
   - *Inadequate/incomplete material models.*
3. Other weaknesses in the programs included:
   - *Poor documentation.*
   - *User unfriendliness*
   - *Limitations in capability of the program to represent actual structures (e.g., they do not represent three dimensional cases and/or do not accept large displacements).*
4. The results of structural analyses in fire are very sensitive to the temperature state of the structure. Many works do not appear to give sufficient importance to this fact. It is therefore essential that accurate thermal predictions are obtained.
5. The effect of stress history on the stress-strain relation of concrete during heating has been proven to be of significance by various experimental studies. This effect has frequently been ignored by most structural programs.
6. There has been a tendency in the majority of the surveyed models to ignore the transient thermal creep in the constitutive model of concrete.

Transitional thermal creep has a significant effect on the behavior of concrete structures under fire, especially in axially loaded members. Therefore, it would be conceptually incorrect to exclude transient thermal creep, although reasonable predictions may be obtained by ignoring its effect in some statically determinate flexural members.

7. The effect of creep on steel at high temperatures appears to be insignificant. This conclusion is in close agreement with those of other research workers in this field.

General Remarks

Most thermal and structural programs appear to have similar theoretical formulations which are technically sound. The difference lies in the material models adopted and in the material data input into the programs. A significant difference between the programs is also in the user-friendliness and documentation of the software, and in most cases the program can only be used effectively by their author.

Since it was found that the majority of available fire-dedicated structural programs still require significant development, and most of these are not user-friendly or properly documented, using them effectively would be very difficult. Such programs cannot be used other than by their own authors and they are, therefore, inadequate as research tools for further development.

REFERENCES

1. M. J. Terro, G. A. Khoury, and P. J. E. Sullivan, *Critical Review of Thermal & Structural Computer Programs—Theory and Practice*, Fire Safety Design Consultants, final report submitted to the Building Research Establishment, February 1991.
2. British Standards Institution, BS 8110:1985, *The Structural Use of Concrete*, Part 2/Section Four.
3. Approved Document B2/3/4, *Fire Spread*, The Building Regulations 1985, Department Of the Environment and The Welsh Office, 1985.
4. R. Iding, B. Bresler, and Z. Nizamuddin, *FIRES-T3, A Computer Program for the Fire Response of Structures—Thermal*, University of California, Berkeley, Fire Research Group, Report No. UCB FRG 77-15, 1977.
5. E. Sterner and U. Wickstrom, *TASEF—Temperature Analysis of Structures Exposed to Fire*, User's Manual, SP Report, 1990:05, Fire Technology, 1990.
6. U. Wickstrom, *TASEF-2, A Computer Program for Temperature Analysis of Structures Exposed to Fire*, Institute of Technology, Lund, 1979.
7. U. Wickstrom, *TASEF v 3.0*, Private Communication, June 1990.
8. Y. Anderberg, *TEMPCALC*, Private Communication, July 1990.
9. Y. Anderberg, *Numerical Modelling of Structures at Elevated Temperatures*, A report submitted to the Fire Research Station by FSD AB, IDEON, 223 70 Lund, Sweden, June 1990.

10. Institute of Fire Safety Design (IFSD), *TEMPCALC User Manual*, IFSD, Lund, IDEON, Sweden, 1986.
11. Ove Arup & Partners (OAP), *Large Panel Systems—Prediction of Behaviour in Fire Tests*, A report submitted by OAP to the Building Research Establishment, Report No. 14404/JB/CW, Building Research Station in June 1985.
12. R. Hass, Computer Models and Simplified Methods for Calculation of Structural Elements under Fire Attack (STABA-F), in *New Technology to Reduce Fire Losses and Costs*, S. J. Grayson and D. A. Smith (eds.), pp. 178–185, 1986.
13. K. Rudolph, E. Richter, R. Hass, and U. Quast, *Principles for Calculation of Load-Bearing and Deformation Behaviour of Composite Structural Elements under Fire Action* (STABA-F), Fire Safety Science, Proceedings of 1st International Symposium, 1986.
14. J. M. Franssen, *Étude du Comportement au Feu des Structures Mixtes Acier-Béton* (CEFICOSS), A Study of the Behaviour of Composite Steel-Concrete Structures in Fire, Thèse de Doctorat, Université de Liège, Belgique, 1987.
15. M. J. Terro, *Numerical Modelling of Thermal & Structural Response of Reinforced Concrete Structures in Fire*, PhD thesis, Department of Civil Engineering, Imperial College of Science, Technology and Medicine, January 1991.
16. J. Wiss and (WJE) Elstner, *FASBUS-II*, A Report Submitted by WJE to the American Iron and Steel Institute on the Assessment and Improvement of FASBUS in 1978.
17. R. Iding, B. Bresler, and Z. Nizamuddin, *FIRES-RCII, A Computer Program for the Fire Response of Structures—Reinforced Concrete Frames*, Fire Research Group, Report No. UCB FRG 77-8, University of California, Berkeley, July 1977.
18. J. Becker and B. Bresler, *FIRES-RC, A Computer Program for the Fire Response of Structures—Reinforced Concrete Frames*, Fire Research Group, Report No. UCB FRG 74-3, University of California, Berkeley, July 1974.
19. J. M. Becker, H. Bizri, and B. Bresler, *FIRES-T, A Computer Program for the Fire Response of Structures—Thermal*, Fire Research Group, Research No. UCB FRG 74-1, University of California, Berkeley, 1974.
20. N. E. Forsen, *A Theoretical Study on the Fire Resistance of Concrete Structures'—CONFIRE*, Cement and Concrete Research Institute, SINTEF Report No. STF65 A82062, The Norwegian Institute of Technology, December 1982.
21. N. E. Forsen, *STEELFIRE—Finite Element Program for Nonlinear Analysis of Steel Frames Exposed to Fire*, Multiconsult AS Consulting Engineers, Norway, September 1983.
22. E. Aldstedt, *Nonlinear Analysis of Reinforced Concrete Frames*, Report No. 75-1, Division of Structural Mechanics, The Norwegian Institute of Technology, The University of Trondheim, March 1975.
23. K. Towler, *Furnace Testing Exposed What is the Alternative?*, A report submitted to the Fire Research Station in the United Kingdom in April 1990.
24. K. Towler, G. Khoury, and P. Sullivan, *Computer Modelling of the Effect of Fire on Large Panel Structures*, Final Report Submitted to the Department Of the Environment by Fire Safety Design Consultants United Kingdom, March 1989.
25. K. Chung, *BFIRE*, The Steel Construction Institute, Private Communication, October 1990.
26. LUSAS, *Advanced Procedures Training Course*, FEA, United Kingdom, 1988.

27. LUSAS, *Examples Manual*, FEA, United Kingdom, 1991.
28. LUSAS, *Mystro User Manual*, FEA, United Kingdom, 1991.
29. LUSAS, *User Manual*, FEA, United Kingdom, 1992.
30. D. A. Nethercott, (University of Sheffield), Private Communication, 1st August 1988 and 20th August 1990.
31. W. Yong, (Building Research Establishment (BRE)), Private Communication, 1990.
32. N. Jeyarupalingam and K. S. Virdi, *Steel Beams and Columns Exposed to Fire Hazard*, A paper to be submitted for presentation at the International Seminar on Design of Structures for Hazardous Loading in April 1991, Structures on Research Centre, Department of Civil Engineering, City University, London.
33. K. S. Virdi, *Validation of Computer Model for Predicting the Structural Response of Steel I-Section Columns Heated Non-Uniformly to Elevated Temperatures*, Report submitted under contract to the Building Research Establishment (Fire Research Station), Report 042.908.01, Department of Civil Engineering, City University, London, August 1988.

CHAPTER 2

Reliability and Computer Models

Alan N. Beard

General categories are identified which indicate possible sources of error in the process of using a computer model to predict the value of a state-variable. Such a state-variable might be, for example, temperature during fire growth in a compartment. It is not the intention to imply that these categories are the only possible ones. It is hoped, however, that this chapter will help to clarify the nature of *error* in the use of computer models and indicate areas for possible future work. The ideas are general and not restricted to fire models.

There has been much development of deterministic computer-based models for fire growth in compartments over the last decade or so [1]. In particular, two types of models have been developed, that is, zone models and field models. Models of this kind are intended to predict values of variables such as temperature and heat flux during compartment fires. The development of such models has raised the question of to what extent they may be regarded as reliable and a debate about the limitations of models of fire growth is in progress [2]. It has been suggested that an independent Model Examination Group be brought into existence in order to examine computer models in the field of fire growth [3, 4]. The identification of sources of error in the process of using a model is a part of this debate. The remainder of this chapter offers a very general categorization which is intended to help stimulate discussion and further work.

RELIABILITY AND COMPUTER MODELS

The reliability of a system or process may be regarded as the probability that performance is equal to requirement, that is,

$$\text{Reliability} = \text{Prob}(\text{Performance} = \text{Requirement})$$

This may be regarded as a general statement and is useful as a definition even if *probability* is not interpreted in strict quantitative terms. It raises the question of what is the *requirement* and what is the *performance* in a particular case. Overall, the requirement may be very complex, as may the performance. In this chapter these terms are being interpreted in relatively simple ways. The requirement is taken to be the demand that using a model enables the actual value of a state-variable, say temperature in a compartment fire, to be predicted. That is, the requirement is that the predicted temperature corresponds to the *real temperature* in a given case. *Real temperature* is meant to imply the actual temperature in a fire which the modeler is attempting to simulate.

CATEGORIZATION OF ERRORS

A categorization of possible sources of error is summarized in the diagram of Figure 1. The vertical line corresponds to a scale for a state-variable, for example the average temperature at a given time of the upper smoke layer resulting from a fire in a compartment. The first point to note is that the state-variable itself may depend upon the assumptions of the model (e.g., average layer temperature results from making a zonal assumption). However, this facet will not be dwelt upon. For a particular fire there will be an actual average upper layer temperature, where the depth of the layer is given by a definition of some kind. (Again, there is a

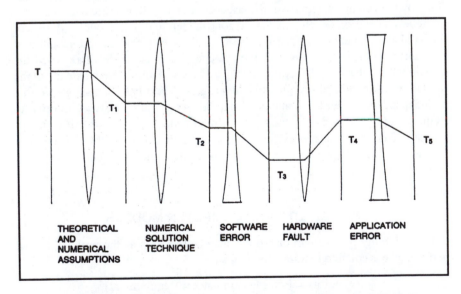

Figure 1. Symbolic representation of sources of error during a calculation.
(T = real temperature; T_5 = temperature calculated.)

dependency upon assumptions made; here, on the definition of layer depth. This, also, will not be dwelt upon.)

In attempting to predict this temperature using a model the primary categories of error may be seen as due to:

- Unreality of the theoretical and numerical assumptions in the model.
- The numerical solution techniques.
- Software error. That is, mistakes in the software, given the theoretical structure and the solution methods. This should also be taken to include possible mistakes in associated software, such as a compiler.
- Hardware Faults.
- Application of the software by a particular user.

Beyond this, the only way we can have knowledge of a *real* temperature, T, is to conduct an experiment. However, the results from an experiment depend upon the experimental design, experimental error and other factors. The experimental T will not, in general, correspond to the actual T and this is represented in Figure 2. To the above set of categories should be added, therefore, the category corresponding to uncertainty associated with experimental results as experiment is the only way we can obtain an approximation to a *real* T. However, Figure 1 is the one which is more directly related to the use of a computer model to make a prediction.

Each of the categories has been modeled, metaphorically, as a lens which produces a shift in the value of T at that stage. No significance should be attached

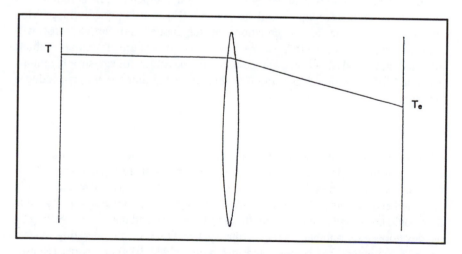

Figure 2. Symbolic representation of error due to experiment.
(T = real temperature; T_e = temperature derived from experiment.)

to the use of convex or concave lenses; the intention is simply to symbolically indicate a shift in T on the scale.

While the actual temperature is indicated by the point, T, on the left hand side, the value predicted, T_5, is on the extreme right hand side. Each of the categories will be considered, briefly, in turn.

Unreality of Theoretical and Numerical Assumptions

A theoretical model can only ever represent an approximation to the real world; at most. A model is constructed by a modeler and is relative to that person's outlook and position; it cannot be absolute. That is, a model is inevitably unrealistic in one way or another. A quantitative model is, in general, a complex of conceptual and numerical assumptions and these assumptions need to be under continual examination. Further, the conceptual categories constructed within a model tend to determine the way we look at the real world and how we test the model. For example, an experimental measurement of the wavelength of red light only has meaning if we have a wave theory of light. If we had a particle theory of the nature of light then the concept of wavelength would have no meaning and there would be no sense in measuring the *wavelength*. In the case of fire therefore, the temperature predicted by a model will inevitably not be the *real* temperature. Let us say the *lens* due to the model itself predicts a value of T_1 rather than the actual value of T.

Numerical Solution Techniques

If the model is complicated enough to require a computer in its solution then numerical solution techniques will be needed. These techniques will provide approximate solutions to the equations of the model and further error will come in here. It is also the case that a solution procedure itself may exhibit untoward numerical behavior, even including the possibility of catastrophic jumps or chaos [5, 6]. Let us say that the *lens* due to the solution technique produces a temperature of T_2.

Software Error

On top of this is the possibility that the software is not an accurate representation of the model and solution procedure. That is, there is the possibility of mistakes existing in the software. It has been estimated that, typically, there could be around eight errors per thousand lines of code and even for safety-critical code there could be around four errors per thousand lines [7]; and that after checking by the developer. As another example, the system OS/360, an operating system for IBM computers, has been quoted as having "about 1000 errors per release" [8, p. 1]. A compiler may also contain errors.

Let it be assumed, therefore, that software error produces a value of T_3.

Hardware Faults

Concern has been expressed about the seemingly increasing lack of reliability of the design of micro-processors due to their sheer complexity [9]. The view has even been expressed that during the 1990's people will be "killed or injured as a pretty direct effect of either mistakes in complex software or mistakes in the design of micro-chips" [10]. Assume that T_4 results.

Errors in Application by a User

Some models are very simple and easy to apply so that mistakes in application are unlikely. In the case of computer-based models this is often not the case. The user may not actually put in what it is intended to put in. For example, the user may put an unintended number in a particular place as input. Further, errors in using software are part of a current study in relation to the use of programs as part of structural analysis [11]. The point, however, is general. Suppose that application error produces a value of T_5.

On top of this is the issue of possible mis-interpretation of the results from a computer model, regardless of possible application errors; that is, inappropriate use. That is a vital but different matter which has been considered to some extent elsewhere [2] and will not be discussed here.

COMPARISON WITH EXPERIMENTAL RESULTS

The calculated value for a state-variable such as temperature cannot be compared directly with the actual temperature in a fire. The best that can be done is to compare with experimental results. That may sound simple but in fact it is not. Experimental results are not absolute but relative to a number of factors associated with the experiment, including the experimental design. For example, if it is desired to measure the *average* upper layer temperature then the experimental *average* depends upon where thermo-couples are placed. This matter, also, has been discussed further elsewhere [2].

To be consistent with the lens analogy being used above, the relationship between the *real* temperature and the experimentally measured temperature is represented as in Figure 2. The temperature, T, is seen experimentally as T_e.

Overall, the process of comparison between theory and experiment is very problematic and it is necessary for a methodology to be devised for this part of the process of evaluation of a model [3, 4].

OPEN-NESS OF THE SOURCE CODE

Specifically, source codes for programs used in safety-critical applications should be open to scrutiny by the public in general and the scientific community in particular [12]. This would help to improve the reliability in several ways, including via the attempt to identify programming mistakes in the code.

CONCLUDING COMMENT

Using a computer model to predict a value of a state-variable, such as temperature in a fire, has implicit within it a number of categories associated with error. Each of these categories needs further examination in a particular case. Beyond that there is the question of the relativity of experimental results and the need for an acceptable methodology for comparing theory with experiment. As a part of these considerations the establishment of an independent Model Examination Group would be a desirable development. Overall, a model such as a fire model should only be used in a supportive role. Any results need to be interpreted in the light of the limitations of the model and other knowledge and experience. It is dangerous to do otherwise.

REFERENCES

1. R. Friedman, An International Survey of Computer Models for Fire and Smoke, *Journal of Fire Protection Engineering, 4*, pp. 81-92, 1992.
2. A. N. Beard, Limitations of Computer Models, *Fire Safety Journal, 18*, pp. 375-391, 1992.
3. A. N. Beard, Evaluation of Deterministic Fire Models: Part 1—Introduction, *Fire Safety Journal, 19*, pp. 295-306, 1992.
4. A. N. Beard, On Comparison Between Theory and Experiment, *Fire Safety Journal, 19*, pp. 307-308, 1992.
5. T. Poston and I. Stewart, *Catastrophe Theory and its Applications*, Pitman, London, 1978.
6. A. C. Robin, Newton-Raphson Behaving Chaotically, *Bulletin of the Institute of Mathematics and its Applications, 26*, pp. 34-35, 1990.
7. D. Jackson, Quoted during presentation on *New Developments in Quality Management as a Pre-requisite to Safety*, Safety-Critical Systems Symposium, Bristol, 9-11 February 1993. Organized by the Safety-Critical Systems Club, c/o Centre for Software Reliability, University of Newcastle.
8. R. C. Backhouse, *Program Construction and Verification*, Prentice Hall, Englewood Cliffs, New Jersey, 1986.
9. L. Clifford, When the Chips are Down, *Systems International, 18*, pp. 42-44, 1990.
10. J. Cullyer, Warwick University; quoted in reference [9].
11. A. J. Morris, *Finite Element Safety-Critical Software*, Safety-Critical Systems Symposium, Bristol, 9-11 February, 1993. Organized by the Safety-Critical Systems Club, c/o Centre for Software Reliability, University of Newcastle.
12. A. N. Beard, *Fire Risk Assessment and Computer Source Codes*, Eighth Seminar on Management of Risk in Engineering (MORE-8), Liverpool, 3-4 March, 1992. Etudes et Dossiers No. 170, August 1992. Geneva Association, 18, Chemin Rieu, CH-1208, Geneva.

CHAPTER 3

The Potential of Expert Systems in Fire Safety Evaluation

H. A. Donegan and I. R. Taylor

The chapter describes two prototype expert system applications to assist in the evaluation of dwelling fire safety though the methods used can be generalized to any building where life safety is a primary objective. The first, based on the philosophy of points schemes, demonstrates a system where the knowledge is elicited from expert opinion. The second illustrates an application where the rules are formulated on the basis of published guidelines and the exemplar relates to disabled users' access and egress. The former displays a *what-if* potential for active/passive trade-off between different measures of fire safety while the latter offers an advice domain. The chapter includes a discussion on the choice of system and its implementation in each case.

GENERAL PRINCIPLES

Risk and Safety Evaluation

In general terms, safety can be viewed naively as the mirror image of risk. The latter unlike the former has a rigorous basis in the theory of probability [1, 2] from which measures can be estimated to cast light on the experts' perception of safety, but there is no such status as *safe*; it is an abstract term. Its intuitive optimum is therefore achieved only by a heuristic minimization of unwanted consequences, that is, by a strategic reduction of evaluated risk. To assume that somehow, absolute safety can be achieved by avoiding all risk is at most naive. In the real world, all that can be achieved is to exchange one level of risk for another of lower level.

This argument provides the philosophical basis for the notion of passive/active trade-off, a key feature in the first expert system example. Later in the chapter a distinction will be made between risk estimation and risk evaluation. Figure 1 attempts to capture the risk domain as *where we are* and the safety domain as *where we would like to be* [3].

Fire safety evaluation with regard to dwellings has received growing attention over the past decade—indeed the current UK legislation requiring the installation of smoke alarms in new and rehabilitated housing stock is some evidence of its impact on government. Moreover it is a recognition of the value of an indigenous active system in the domestic environment and opens the potential for engineering solutions involving trade-off.

The Captivation of Expertise

Fire safety research concerns itself with a number of discrete areas which contribute to the overall expertise of architects, surveyors, engineers, building control officers and the newly emerging fire safety technologists. However, notwithstanding the work of FORUM [4], the complexity of modern buildings makes it almost impossible for these professionals to cope with the volume of "research into practice" which is necessary for either the support of engineering solutions or compliance with legislation. Given the emerging statistically stable level of deaths

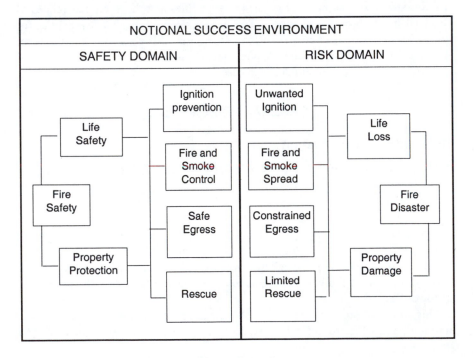

Figure 1. Simple fire safety system.

due to fire (approximately 800 per annum in the UK)—the rewards for such a burden of responsibility are barely tangible. For example, the motivation to improve building design from a fire safety point of view is seldom the number one priority of an architect. Such motivation, if any, will emerge only from the necessity to appease government and public anxiety as a result of the so-called multiple death scenario. It is therefore likely that, given the present stable death rate due to fire, the best that can be hoped for in any new approach to design is a reduction in the frequency of multiple death tragedies or, from a property protection objective, a significant saving on structural cost. It is important therefore to find a way forward that reduces this burden of expertise and fortunately the technology is available in the form of expert systems.

Trends in Computing

In parallel with the developments in fire engineering there has been a remarkable overall trend in the utilization of computer technology. The evidence is revealed in the proceedings *inter alia* of the three major international symposia on fire safety science [5–7]. This emphasis on computing is to be applauded, but not at the expense of confusing the real objectives. The cult of developing sophisticated models as an exercise in software engineering, notwithstanding the demands of reality, should not be encouraged within the world of fire engineering. With increasing numbers of software users among the fire engineering community, considerable care will be needed to distinguish fad from necessity. Such challenges of academic demarcation are not without precedent—the established history of tensions between the competing fields of pure and applied mathematics is probably the nearest analogy.

Research into practice suggests a further note of caution; fire engineering software tools could quite easily be regarded as a panacea by even experienced, possibly beguiled, users. If the panacea is ever realized then it will surely emanate from one of the "dreams" of artificial intelligence (AI), *viz.* the creation of a universal problem solver. A general problem solver is essentially a program that yields solutions when given a variety of different problems about which it has no specific (designed-in) knowledge. The considerable literature on AI illustrates quite clearly why this dream is as tantalizing as it is difficult to realize. Nevertheless, the advancement of Information Systems is such that retrospective viewing of the major symposia ten years from now will reveal a significant impact of AI on FSE.

Traditionally there are two types of problems—the first one can be solved using deterministic methods, for example, determining the flame height for a specific heat source over time. The techniques used to solve these types of problems are easily translated to algorithms which are traditionally executed on computer. The second type of problem does not readily lend itself to this type of computational solution—for example, the assessment of a building with respect to egress for disabled occupants. Such problems are solved by searching for a solution. It is this method of problem solving that AI is concerned with.

According to Hatvany, AI involves "broadening our computer approach from algorithmic thinking to nonalgorithmic thinking and combining the two" [8]. This is readily accommodated in one of the important consequences of AI—expert systems. Briefly, these are interactive computer programs constructed around "rules" and so called "know-how" obtained from experience.

Expert systems are concerned with manipulating knowledge rather than data. The corresponding programs comprise a series of heuristics—a computer scientist's term for rules-of-thumb. These are bits of "know-how" based on human knowledge and tradition making fire engineering with its legislative envelope a natural candidate for this type of treatment. Essentially, legislation is a distillation of experience but with the proviso that it is not infallible. This leaves considerable scope for an expert system to combine rules of tradition with engineering rules of performance.

At the heart of most expert systems produced so far is a *shell* providing an interface with the user, a means to represent knowledge and an ability to reason with the knowledge. The more complex the shell the more versatile the system. Moreover, a complex shell provides greater flexibility in the manipulation of rules and creates a corresponding capability to harness ancillary software for the enhancement of applications.

The following sections detail the development of the present systems, one with regard to trade-off in passive/active fire safety evaluation and the other in respect of disabled occupancy. The latter is clearly related to the life safety objective whereas the former relates directly to both property protection and life safety and indirectly to prevention of conflagration.

Incorporation of Expertise

In Fire Safety Engineering there are three accepted primary objectives, life safety, property protection and prevention of conflagration. These are not necessarily independent attributes but each has a different mode of visualization or measurement. Life safety, for example, is concerned with occupants being exposed to fire hazard and having enough time to evacuate a threatened area whereas property protection is concerned with the building fabric and the contents. The third objective relates quite significantly to both but is primarily concerned with making sure that a fire threat remains indigenous to source.

With a focus on these objectives, expert systems both directly and indirectly have a major part to play, and knowledge capture is of paramount importance to their effectiveness. Expert opinion achieved through consensus in a developing field must undoubtedly rate the highest priority, as the mean age of the experts is in the upper quartile [9]. The problems of collecting such soft data have been addressed by Shields et al. [10] and Marchant [11]. Clearly the same urgency is not applicable in cases where relevant hard data is readily available, for example, raw statistics, thermodynamic formulae, and well established priorities.

Such a background demands a strategic approach to safety or risk evaluation. Unlike risk estimation which requires a reliable database of statistical data risk evaluation, relying on social and political judgments, is aimed at determining the importance of hazards and the risk of harm to those exposed to the hazard. Nelson and Shibe were the first to produce a fire safety evaluation scheme, directed at health care facilities in the United States [12]. Marchant followed this with a fire safety evaluation points scheme for patient areas within hospitals [13] and using the same hierarchical philosophy, Shields et al. developed a points scheme for dwellings [14]. The theoretical consequences [15, 16] and practical considerations [17] of the latter provide the immediate environment for the first expert system example.

EXAMPLE ONE

Theoretical Background

The ideas in [13] and [14] are directed toward the production of a prioritized set of (11 in this case) fire safety component weightings $w_1 \geq w_2 \geq ..\geq w_{11}$ denoted by:

$$V' = (w_1, w_2, w_3, ... w_{11})$$

and referred to as the priority vector. Henceforth the components will be identified by their positions in the priority vector, viz. $C_1, C_2, C_3, ..., C_{11}$. Typical components in the Shields et al. study are fire brigade, occupants and visitors, contents, management, detection systems, fire fighting equipment and so on [14]. The weightings emerge from the consensus [18, 19] of expert opinion derived from a Delphi [20] data collection process (see Figure 2).

Expert opinion at a local level is used to obtain the so-called norm scores for a specific dwelling type. These scores are decided upon by, for example, housing committees or associations so that they have a basis of fire safety comparison for corresponding dwellings within their control. The consensus scores for C_1, C_2 etc. are determined using the methods outlined in [17] and are represented by V_N where,

$$V_N = (q_1, q_2, q_3, ... q_{11})$$

For an actual dwelling the safety of which is to be appraised, a trained surveyor using the same scoring scheme produces a corresponding set of survey scores V_s where,

$$V_s = (s_1, s_2, s_3, ... s_{11})$$

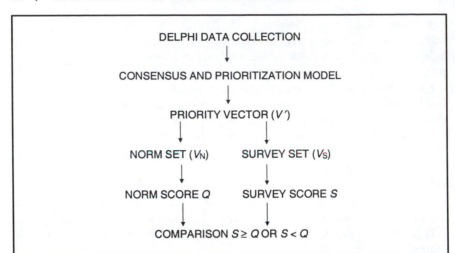

Figure 2. Generalized evaluation framework.

The survey scores are weighted by the entries from the priority vector V' and compared with the similarly weighted norm scores as additive value functions thus:

$$V' \cdot V_s = \sum_i w_i s_i = S \qquad (1)$$

$$V' \cdot V_N = \sum_i w_i q_i = Q \qquad (2)$$

Basically, if $S < Q$ then the dwelling fails to meet the required standard and must therefore be improved with respect to fire safety. The difficulties under a manual system in making the necessary improvement are self evident. An expert system offering a *what if* facility is a natural step given the knowledge capture implicit in both the priority vector and the set of norm scores. The inherent consistency of the system (for a given knowledge base) means that experiments can be performed with logical repeatability.

System Implementation for Example One

Within the constraints of existing legislation, consideration is being given to engineering strategies which will facilitate a degree of trade-off between passive and active fire safety measures. The advantage of the above generalization overcomes the drawback of the manual system in that it is quite feasible for a dwelling to satisfy the overall criterion, viz: $S > Q$ and yet fail in one or more subsets of the components. Given that there are $(2^n - 1)$ mathematically possible subsets for the n components this can lead to a large number of possibilities for large n. However in this case with n = 11 [17], it is feasible to cluster the components from a fire engineering point of view as follows:

A. Human measures—occupancy related
B. Passive measures—building specific
C. Supportive measures—intrinsic and extrinsic

The eleven components are structured within the three measures as shown in the knowledge map, Figure 3, with active, as opposed to passive, measures being subdivided into the human and the supportive measures. With knowledge contained in the selection and prioritization of components, their relative weightings and corresponding norm scores it is clear that an expert system must incorporate this information in a structured manner. Based on the theoretical background and the introduction to this section, a user of the system will, as a minimum expect it to:

1. decide overall if a dwelling is adequate in terms of fire safety,
2. allow a degree of trade-off between the different components of fire safety,
3. allow for changes in the dwelling specification to test *what if* questions,
4. answer *why* questions to justify its conclusions.

Furthermore the guaranteed consistency allows a variety of people in different locations to access its expertise. By building in help information at various levels, the system can be employed by more users allowing them to learn from the inbuilt

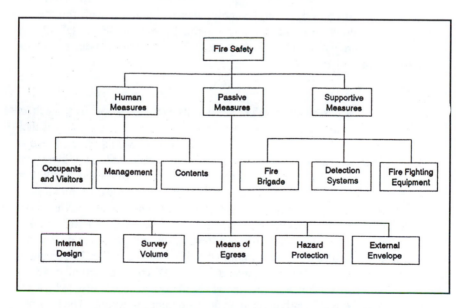

Figure 3. External knowledge map.

expertise. To enable such use, information about the dwelling under consideration must be input, with the system asking appropriate questions and using default values if no information is available.

The Shell

An expert system requires a knowledge base within which expertise is represented, an inference engine to process the knowledge and an interface to users and developers. In testing the feasibility of an application it is desirable to use an expert system shell to assist the formulation of the program, as against using a language such as Prolog or Lisp. Though constrained in adaptability, such a shell is much faster to implement. It already contains the inference engine to process the knowledge together with an interface for both building and using the system. The knowledge itself can be structured by a variety of methods, for example, rules, frames, or semantic nets. Since the shell is *domain-free*, the knowledge base contains all the expertise of the system, which as well as rules and facts includes appropriate questions to and help for the user. In this particular example the PC version of the rule based shell Xi Plus is used [21]. The shell accommodates links to, for example, databases, spreadsheets, and C programs and this feature is utilized for some of the data. The shell provides a comprehensive set of tools for developing and testing the knowledge base, within a user friendly environment. While it does not allow for probabilities within the data this is not necessary in the present study.

Relatively little work on the application of expert systems within fire safety has been published, with most of it on the compliance of buildings with fire regulations. The best known example is the commercial program BRIGADE [22], a system with 4000 rules based on the shell Level 5, while there are discussions of ongoing work in [23] and [24].

The Strategy

In the system as described in [17], worksheets were used to assess each of components with a rating on a scale from zero to five. Each survey set V_s was then weighted by the priority vector V' to give an overall score S on a scale of zero to 500. Expert opinion indicates that for the house type considered in the investigation, a norm score, Q of 375 or 75 percent would be sufficient for the dwelling to satisfy fire safety standards. This equates with norm scores for each measure of (A,154), (B,154) and (C,67), each being 75 percent of the corresponding maximum allocations of (A,205), (B,205) and (C,90). To allow for trade-off or compensation between the different measures a lower minimum score for A, B and C must be decided, again by expert opinion, with this value less than 75 percent of the overall maximum allocation, as illustrated in the Discussion section, p. 43

Within the expert system separate knowledge bases were constructed for the three measures A, B and C, aiding separate development and testing. The information required is obtained by prompting the user with various questions. The answers fire the inbuilt rules of the knowledge base and along with other information stored as data the program decides on an overall score for the dwelling.

Unlike the manual system, the expert system can allow different levels of trade-off between A, B and C by setting separate norms for these measures. For example, in obtaining a rating for *means of egress* the information considered is (i) the distance to an exit, (ii) whether or not escape routes are protected and (iii) the potential for rescue. A screen of the form of Figure 4 is used to request information, with help available if required. Within this component there are rules such as:

IF dwelling is single storey
     and route is unprotected
     and travel distance < 15
     and travel distance ≥ 10
THEN escape potential score = 1.7

IF escape potential score ≥ 0
     and rescue potential score ≥ 0
THEN means of egress score = round (escape potential score * rescue potential
     score, 4)

where the final rule above combines escape and rescue potential scores and rounds the answer to four decimal places. There are a total of 36 rules for the *means of egress* component.

Under A for human measures there are forty-six rules, in B on passive measures there are eighty rules with thirty-four rules in C. To test a system with a total of 160 rules, as many as possible paths through the system must be tried. A set of test cases representing standard and extreme situations was developed, to probe the system for potential limitations and weaknesses.

Discussion

In applying the program to an actual dwelling, typical output as illustrated in Example 1 might be

Example 1

	actual score	minimum pass with trade-off	normal pass	pass/fail
A: Human Measures	163	133	154	pass
B: Building Specific Measures	161	133	154	pass
C: Supportive Measures	63	59	67	trade-off
Overall	**387**		**375**	**pass**

Application: fire in the home
Knowledgebase: Passive Measures

Means of Egress

What is the greatest distance travelled (in metres) from any habitable room within the survey volume to a storey exit?	8
Is the escape route protected or unprotected?	◊ protected unprotected

Tab/Backtab next/previous field

Esc cancel || Ctrl+Rtn end || F3 why || Rtn select ||

Figure 4. Information requested on means of egress,
within passive measures.

To allow for trade-off between the different measures, the minimum allowed scores for A, B and C have to be less than 75 percent of their respective maxima, where 75 percent is the overall percentage required. The amount of trade-off or compensation can be decided by the local experts and in these examples has been set to allow trade-off down to 65 percent of each measure maximum. In the above example trade-off is occurring between C, (below the normal pass level) and A and B to give an overall pass for the dwelling.

In contrast for another dwelling the results may be:

Example 2

	actual score	minimum pass with trade-off	normal pass	pass/fail
A: Human Measures	152	133	154	trade-off
B: Building Specific Measures	143	133	154	trade-off
C: Supportive Measures	72	59	67	pass
Overall	**367**		**375**	**fail**

so that the dwelling fails to reach the required overall standard even though it passes in C and is above the minimum pass with trade-off in A and B. If trade-off is allowed, by setting the minimum standard for A, B and C separately below the overall standard required, then inevitably some dwellings will pass with tradeoff in some aspects but fail to reach the required overall standard, as in this example.

In summary, when trade-off is in operation, a building may pass by being above the norm score in each measure or pass with trade-off (Example 1) if the compensating measure scores are high enough. Conversely, a building may fail with trade-off if compensating measures are insufficient to counterbalance the deficiencies of the lower scores, as in Example 2. By setting the minimum allowed scores for A, B and C at 154, 154 and 67 respectively, that is, 75 percent of each maximum possible score of 205, 205 and 90, no trade-off would be allowed between the measures. The philosophy of trade-off is discussed further by Harmathy [25] and from a probabilistic point of view by Ramachandran in [26].

If a dwelling fails to reach the overall standard, the expert system allows a *what-if* type investigation to be performed to ascertain what improvements may be made to bring the house up to specification. With the addition of some financial information the alternate cost of a range of possible alterations to the building may be explored using the expert system. The program can be easily adjusted to allow trade-off only between the passive and supportive measures, B and C.

EXAMPLE TWO

Assessment of Buildings for Use by Disabled People

While this example relates particularly to the United Kingdom its methods may be generalized to any situation where well-defined rules and guidelines are in existence. Since 1970 there has been a growing recognition of the place and needs of disabled people in the community coupled with a parallel development in legislation and codes of practice. For example in the United Kingdom the 1970 Chronically Sick and Disabled Persons Act [27] made provision in the construction of new public assembly buildings or the modification of existing buildings for the needs of members of the public who are disabled. Further legislation followed extending the requirements to places of employment [28], to educational buildings [29] and to other buildings to which the public are admitted [30]. Codes of practice were published to guide architects in its implementation, much of it being based on the earlier work of Goldsmith [31]. However the above developments were primarily concerned with access into buildings and ease of use for disabled people within them.

The converse process, of egress or evacuation under emergency conditions, was not seriously addressed in the United Kingdom until 1988 when Part 8 of BS5588 was published [32]. This code of practice provides designers with guidance on the incorporation of measures in new or existing buildings to enable safe evacuation of people with disabilities. This code of practice is the culmination of earlier work by Marchant [33], Archea and Margulis [34], Johnson [35] and Pearson and Joost [36]. Nelson [37] addresses the concern in the United States for egress of disabled people while Shields [38] includes a comprehensive review of the literature to date.

In such an expanding area of knowledge, problems arise for architects in designing general purpose buildings which must allow for use by people with a variety of disabilities. Designers may also be involved in the conversion of existing buildings which again must take account of any special provision for disabled people. It may be unreasonable for such an architect to be an expert on all the aspects of current legislation in this field. The purpose of this application of an expert system is to indicate the potential for such programs to assist a designer by providing expert knowledge of what is required to allow for the particular needs of disabled people. Such needs may be with respect to normal access to a building, ease of use within it or egress in emergency situations.

To demonstrate the potential of such a system the present project has concentrated on the conversion of existing dwellings for use by disabled people.

Characteristics of Disabled Population

People classified as disabled exhibit a wide range of differing abilities with respect to their mobility with consequent levels of difficulty in, for example, gaining access to a building, moving around a home or in their own self care. A recent survey [39] of one group of handicapped people showed that 44 percent had difficulty with stairs, 32 percent with using the bath and 11 percent with moving around on the level. While 5 percent of the survey expressed the need for rehousing in more appropriate accommodation most required lesser modifications to their present home. Such diversity of need cannot be catered for by one model of housing adaptation. Instead modifications to any house for use by a disabled person must be made after taking account of the context of the proposed resident. A decision must then be made as to the feasibility of adapting the house or of moving the disabled person to one more suitable to their level of mobility. Other considerations in such a decision will include the life expectancy of the disabled person and whether or not their mobility will degenerate further as a result of illness. In making such decisions an architect or estate manager will normally be involved as one member of an assessment team. However, such a person cannot be expected to be fully conversant with all the possible problems. To show the possibilities of advice and guidance from an expert system this pilot program has been designed.

For the purpose of this study the disabled population has been divided into those who require *Mobility Housing* and those who need *Wheelchair Housing*. O'Connor [40] has defined the former group as requiring "ordinary housing modified to be more convenient for disabled people to move about and live in."

Such housing is appropriate for the ambulant disabled with mobility problems and wheelchair users who can stand to transfer and walk a few steps. Attention must be paid to accessible entrances, internal dimensions and use of facilities on the entrance level. Wheelchair housing is more appropriate for those who are confined to a wheelchair, people with deteriorating conditions who may become wheelchair-bound or those who need a wheelchair for access to, say kitchen or bathroom facilities.

Bearing in mind the above needs of disabled people the system developed to date has concentrated on access to and egress from the building itself, the general circulation areas, kitchen and bath or shower rooms. The analysis is limited to dwellings on a single level.

The system is designed to guide an architect through these aspects of a proposed house for a disabled person and allow an informed decision as to whether the house is suitable, requires minor or major modifications or is unsuitable. It can also be used in single room mode to enable an assessment to be performed for one facility of the house.

Knowledge Base Structures

Since the knowledge required to assess the suitability of a house under the above areas falls into mutually exclusive categories it was decided to structure the overall knowledge base into sections based on access, kitchen, bathroom and shower room. It is assumed that only one of the last two facilities is assessed in any given house. Finally the questions and assessment depend on the mobility of the disabled person as to which kind of housing—mobility housing or wheelchair housing is required. The overall knowledge base structure is shown in Figure 5. The knowledge base sections for Wheelchair Housing are based on those for Mobility Housing but with further more restrictive rules. The "house" module coordinates an overall assessment for the building but also allows the user to request an assessment of one aspect of the building only.

Each section of the knowledge base contains rules which enable an appropriate assessment of the building to be made. For example the access knowledge base contains a number of rules on whether or not a ramp can be provided or its present suitability, for example

IF a ramp is nonexistent
    and enough space is available
    THEN a new ramp is possible.
IF a ramp is in existence
    and ramp gradient is less than 1 in 12
    and ramp fall is across the tread
    and ramp rest platforms are at doors and direction changes
    and ramp gaps are at adjacent walls
    THEN ramp is suitable

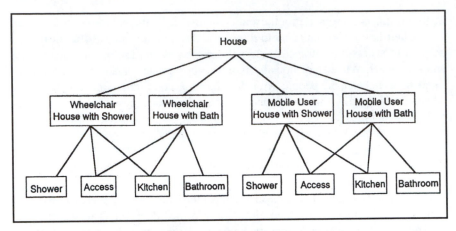

Figure 5. Assessment of housing for disabled people—
knowledge base structure.

with further rules on handrails, kerbs, adhesion, and provision of gulleys for drainage. The system then examines access through doorways and internal passage-ways. Based on the above information the access knowledge base decides if access provision is suitable, suitable with minor or major modifications or is unsuitable. The information required is obtained from the user through computer forms with an example shown in Figure 6, requesting information on an existing ramp.

An overall assessment of the house is based on separate assessments for the three areas of access, kitchen and bath or shower room. The scale of modifications and the number of areas in which they are required determines the overall clas-sification as illustrated in Table 1.

Results and Discussion

As indicated in Figure 6 the user can ask why a particular question is required, with the knowledge base replying with information on how the response will assist in making an assessment. Having made an assessment the user may then ask *what if* type questions to modify previous information given to the knowledge base and hence investigate the effect of possible improvements to the building. With further development the system could be used on site to make an immediate assessment of a building. Additional on-line help could enhance the system as a training tool or allow those with less expertise to make initial assessments.

CONCLUSION

In conclusion these examples show the potential for the application of knowledge-based systems to fire safety issues. Both examples involve the assessment of

Application: Housing Knowledgebase: Access	
Ramp Properties	
Is the ramp gradient?	less than 1 in 12 greater than 1 in 12
Is the ramp fall?	across the trad non-existent
Are ramp gaps?	at adjacent walls absent
Are there ramp rest platforms?	at doors and direction changes absent
	Tab/Backtab next/previous field
Esc cancel || Ctrl+Rtn end || F3 why || Rtn select ||	

Figure 6. Information on ramp properties.

Table 1.

Knowledge Base Sections	Overall Assessment
All suitable	Suitable
One or two minor modifications, one suitable	Suitable with minor modifications
Three minor modification two major modifications	Suitable with major modification
Three major modifications Any section unsuitable	Unsuitable

buildings, the first with direct application to fire safety and the second less directly in its examination of buildings for disabled people. Of course the two assessments can be combined to provide an appraisal of a potential house for a disabled person with respect to fire safety. The programs illustrate the merits of using an expert system shell to encapsulate the knowledge, especially in comparison to using a conventional programming language. The program can be run at all stages of development and provides a built in user friendliness. On any consultation context sensitive help is available to the user at the level required, the user may ask the system why some information is required and may explore *what if* type situations. When run in a portable PC, the programs could be employed on-site to assess the status of a dwelling and, if required, to suggest options for improving its level of fire safety to the required level in example one or to suggest possible modifications to its suitability for disabled persons. The first program shows the effect of trade-off between different aspects of fire safety, but the amount of trade-off may be adjusted. In contrast the second example, still in its development phase shows how the requirements of different modules of the knowledge base may be combined. On the basis of these pilot studies the authors are convinced that expert systems incorporating a specific knowledge base have potential to assist experts and others in the assessment of buildings. Work is ongoing to incorporate directly into the programs the knowledge of the building structure required, using an interface to the databases produced in Computer Aided Designs.

REFERENCES

1. J. R. Hall and A. Sekizawa, A Fire Risk Analysis: General Conceptual Framework for Describing Models, *Fire Technology* 27:1, pp. 33-53, 1991.
2. G. Ramachandran, Statistical Methods in Risk Evaluation, *Fire Safety Journal, 2*, pp. 125-145, 1979.
3. I. R. Taylor and H. A. Donegan, *An Application of the Expert System Shell Xi-Plus to Fire Safety Analysis*, ILIAM VIII Proceedings, Dublin City University, pp. 81-89, 1991.
4. J. E. Snell, *International Fire Research*, Fire Safety Science—Proceedings of the Third International Symposium, pp. 149-163, 1991.
5. Fire Safety Science—Proceedings of the First International Symposium, 1986.
6. Fire Safety Science—Proceedings of the Second International Symposium, 1989.
7. Fire Safety Science—Proceedings of the Third International Symposium, 1991.
8. J. Hatvany, The Missing Tools of CAD for Mechanical Engineering, in *Knowledge Engineering in Computer-Aided-Design*, J. S. Gero(ed.), Elsevier, 1985.
9. J. McMahon, F. Dodd, I. R. Taylor, and H. A. Donegan, *Fire Modelling—A Postgraduate Student's Perception*, INTERFLAM '93, Proceedings of the Sixth International Fire Conference, pp. 719-728, 1993.
10. T. J. Shields, G. W. Silcock, and H. A. Donegan, Methodological Problems Associated with the Use of the Delphi Technique, *Fire Technology, 23*, pp. 175-186, 1987.
11. E. W. Marchant, Problems Associated with the Delphi Technique, *Fire Technology, 24*:1, pp. 59-62, 1988.
12. H. E. Nelson and A. J. Shibe, *A System of Fire Safety Evaluation of Health Care Facilities*, Report NBSIR 78-1555-1, NBS, 1978.
13. E. W. Marchant (ed.), *Fire Safety Evaluation (Points) Scheme for Patient Areas within Hospitals*, a report on its origins and development sponsored by DHSS Department of Fire Safety Engineering, University of Edinburgh, 1982.

14. T. J. Shields, G. W. Silcock, and Y. Bell, Fire Safety Evaluation of Dwellings, *Fire Safety Journal, 10*, pp. 29-36, 1986.

15. H. A. Donegan, T. J. Shields, and G. W. Silcock, *A Mathematical Strategy to Relate Fire Safety Evaluation and Fire Safety Policy Formulation for Buildings*, Fire Safety Science—Proceedings of the 2nd International Symposium, Tokyo, pp. 433-441, 1988.

16. T. J. Shields, G. W. Silcock, and H. A. Donegan, The Development of a Fire Safety Evaluation Points Scheme for Dwellings, Part I—Some Theoretical Considerations, *Fire Safety Journal, 15*, pp. 313-324, 1989.

17. T. J. Shields, G. W. Silcock, and H. A. Donegan, *Assessing Fire Risk in Dwellings*, University of Ulster, 1989.

18. H. A. Donegan and F. J. Dodd, An Analytical Approach to Consensus, *Applied Mathematics Letters, V4*:2, pp. 21-24, 1991.

19. F. J. Dodd and H. A. Donegan, Comparative and Compound Consensus, *Applied Mathematics Letters, V5*:3, pp. 31-33, 1992.

20. H. A. Linstone and M. Turoff (eds.), *The Delphi Method, Techniques and Applications*, Addison Wesley, 1975.

21. Xi-Plus, Expertech Ltd., Slough, United Kingdom, 1990.

22. Peregrine Expert Systems Ltd., *Brigade*, Dublin, 1988.

23. G. Hamilton, A. P. Harrison, and J. R. Pascall, *Directory of Research and Development of Expert Systems in the Construction and Building Services Industries*, Vol. III, BSRIA Ref 7177, 1983.

24. M. R. Shaw, *Expert Systems and the Construction Industry*, B.R.E. Garston, United Kingdom, 1989.

25. T. Z. Harmathy, A Decision Logic for Trading between Fire Safety Measures, *Fire and Materials, 14*, pp. 1-10, 1989.

26. G. Ramachandran, Trade-Offs between Sprinklers and Fire Resistance, *Fire*, pp. 211-212, 1982.

27. The Chronically Sick and Disabled Persons Act, United Kingdom, 1970.

28. The Chronically Sick and Disabled Persons (Amendment) Act, United Kingdom, 1976.

29. Department of Education and Science, *Access for Disabled People to Educational Buildings*, Design Note 18, London, 1984.

30. The Building (Disabled People) Regulations: Part M, *Access for Disabled People*, London, 1987.

31. S. Goldsmith, *Designing for the Disabled*, RIBA, 1976.

32. British Standards Institution, Fire Precautions in the Design and Construction of Buildings. Part 8. Code of Practice for Means of Escape for Disabled People, *British Standard BS 5588: Part 8*; London, 1988.

33. E. W. Marchant (ed.), *Proceedings of Seminar Fire Safety for the Handicapped*, Edinburgh, 1975.

34. J. Archea and Margulis, *The Evacuation of Non-Ambulatory Patients from Hospital and Nursing Home Fires: A Framework for a Model*, PB80-11950, NBS, 1979.

35. B. Johnson, *Evacuation Techniques for Disabled Persons*, National Research Council of Canada, 13SR-31155-2-3204, Ottawa, 1983.

36. R. G. Pearson and M. G. Joost, *Egress Behaviour Response Times of Handicapped and Elderly Subjects to Simulated Residential Fire Situations*, PB83-222695, NBS, 1983.
37. H. E. Nelson, *Fire Modelling Assessment of Areas of Refuge Intended to Provide Safety for Persons with Mobility Limitations*, Interflam '93, Sixth International Fire Conference, United Kingdom, pp. 161-170, 1993.
38. T. J. Shields, *Fire and Disabled People in Buildings*, Building Research Establishment Report, 1993.
39. M. Smith, P. Robinson, and B. Duffy, *The Prevalence of Disability in Northern Ireland*, Policy Planning and Research Unit, Government of Northern Ireland, 1992.
40. G. O'Connor, *Housing Disabled People—A Design Guide*, Northern Ireland Housing Executive, 1986

CHAPTER 4

A Model of Instability and Flashover

Alan Beard, Dougal Drysdale,
Paul Holborn, and Steven Bishop

A nonlinear model, FLASHOVER A1, is presented within a zonal formulation which may be used to predict the geometrical and thermo-physical conditions which lead to an instability in the system. In particular, the existence of a critical fire radius is demonstrated at which the state becomes unstable. After this point a rapid development to a post-flashover state would be expected, given sufficient fuel and ventilation. In a practical case it would be desirable to attempt to ensure that the fire radius remains below the critical value. In such a way this model may assist in the assessment of a design.

Theoretical models for predicting the conditions which give rise to flashover are desirable in order to assist in assessing the likelihood of flashover in a given case. In principle, with a model, it should be possible to estimate the effect of making alterations to material or geometrical characteristics of a design for a new or existing building. Two theoretical models for predicting flashover, using zonal formulations, have already been described by the authors [1, 2]. These models have applied the concepts of nonlinear dynamics to fire in a compartment. The earlier models assumed one and two state-variables respectively, corresponding to temperature of the upper smoke layer in the first case and upper layer temperature together with fire radius in the second. This article describes a three state-variable model in which a third variable, smoke layer depth, is included.

GENERAL STRUCTURE OF THE MODEL

A zone model has been constructed, as illustrated in Figure 1, which makes the following basic assumptions:

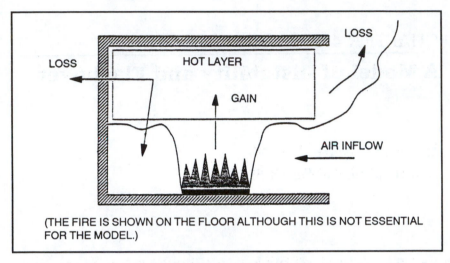

Figure 1. The compartment fire assumed.

- A rectangular cuboidal compartment has been assumed of length L_1, width L_2 and height H. A fire has its base at a distance L_3 below the ceiling.
- There is a single ventilation opening of rectangular shape and width, W, which extends from floor to ceiling.
- A fire of circular perimeter and radius, R, entrains air and produces smoke which rises to form a hot layer of depth, Z, and uniform temperature, T. Smoke is lost through the ventilation opening.
- The lower layer consists of air at ambient temperature.
- The three state-variables for the model are: 1) Temperature of the upper layer, T; 2) Radius of the fire, R; 3) Depth of the upper layer, Z.

Conservation of Energy

Applying the principle of conservation of energy to the upper layer results in the equation:

$$G = \dot{U} + L + \dot{w} \tag{1}$$

where:
G = Rate of gain of energy of the upper layer
L = Rate of loss of energy of the upper layer
$\dot{w}$ = Rate of work done associated with the upper layer
$\dot{U}$ = Rate of change of internal energy of the upper layer

Each of the terms in equation (1) may be broken down as follows:

$$G = \dot{Q}_i + \dot{H}_i \tag{2}$$

where:

$\dot{Q}_i$ = Rate of energy going into the upper layer from the fire; i.e., convected in via the plume together with radiation from the flame.

$\dot{H}_i$ = Enthalpy flow rate into the plume from the lower space gases and the fuel.

$$L = \dot{Q}_o + \dot{H}_o \tag{3}$$

where:

$\dot{Q}_o$ = Rate of energy leaving the upper layer; other than that associated with the smoke flow out of the compartment.

$\dot{H}_o$ = Enthalpy flow rate out of the upper layer through the ventilation opening.

$$\dot{w} = A \, p \, dZ/dt \tag{4}$$

where:

A = Area of the ceiling
p = Pressure within the upper layer
Z = Depth of the upper layer

$$\dot{U} = A \, C_v \, d(\rho T \, Z)/dt \tag{5}$$

where:

C_v = Specific heat at constant volume of the smoke layer gases.
ρ = Density of the upper layer
T = temperature of the upper layer
t = Time

The term $\dot{Q}_o$ of equation (3) may further be de-composed into:

$$\dot{Q}_o = \dot{Q}_{o1} + \dot{Q}_{o2} \tag{6}$$

where:

$\dot{Q}_{o1}$ = Rate of energy loss from the upper layer via radiation to the lower surface and out of the vent. Here, "lower surface" refers to that part of the compartment not in contact with the upper layer; i.e., the floor and the lower parts of the walls. Also, "lower part of the vent" means that part of the vent below the interface.

$\dot{Q}_{o2}$ = Rate of radiative and convective energy loss from the upper layer to the upper surface and out of the upper part of the vent. Here, "upper surface" refers to that part of the compartment in direct contact with the upper layer, i.e., the ceiling and the upper parts of the walls. Also, "upper part of the vent" means that part of the vent above the interface.

Also, the term $\dot{Q}_i$ of equation (2) may be de-composed into:

$$\dot{Q}_i = N_1 \dot{Q}_f \tag{7}$$

where:
$\dot{Q}_f$ = Rate of energy production via combustion.
N_1 = That fraction of $\dot{Q}_f$ which goes into the upper layer.

The heat release rate, $\dot{Q}_f$, is assumed to be given by:

$$\dot{Q}_f = \chi\, \dot{m}_f\, H_c \qquad \text{if } \dot{m}_e\, /\, \dot{m}_f > S_r \tag{8}$$

$$= \chi\, (\dot{m}_e\, /\, S_r)\, H_c \quad \text{if } \dot{m}_e\, /\, \dot{m}_f < S_r \tag{9}$$

where:
χ = Combustion efficiency
$\dot{m}_f$ = Fuel volatilization rate
$\dot{m}_e$ = Rate of entrainment of air
H_c = Heat of combustion
S_r = Stoichiometric ratio

The fuel volatilization rate has been assumed to be governed by the net heat flux to the surface of the pyrolysing fuel, $\dot{q}''$, via:

$$\dot{m}_f = A_f\, \dot{q}'' \,/\, H_v \tag{10}$$

where:
A_f = Surface area of the pyrolysing fuel
$\quad = \pi R^2$; R = Radius of the circular perimeter
$\dot{q}''$ = Net heat flux to the surface of the fuel
H_v = Heat of vaporization of the fuel

The term $\dot{q}''$ includes radiative heat transfer from the upper layer and upper surface of the room to the fuel as well as radiative and convective heat transfer from the flame to the fuel.

Conservation of Mass

Applying the principle of conservation of mass to the upper layer results in the equation:

$$\dot{m}_e + \dot{m}_f = \dot{m}_o + A\, d(\rho Z)/dt \tag{11}$$

where:
$\dot{m}_e$ = Mass flow rate of air entrained from the lower layer
$\dot{m}_o$ = Mass flow rate from the smoke layer out of the vent

The mass flow rate out of the vent has been assumed to be given by the expression of Rockett [3]. The mass flow rate of entrained air has been assumed to be given by the expression of Zukoski [4] in the earlier stages and by the expression of Prahl and Emmons [5] for vent inflow during the latter stages. Further details are given in Appendix 1.

Flame Spread Rate

The rate of change of fire radius has been taken from Emmons [6]:

$$dR/dt = 0.011 \ \Omega \ \{1 + (\Omega/2) + (\Omega^2/3)\} \tag{12}$$

where:

$\Omega = \dot{q}'' / (\sigma \ T_f 4)$; σ = Stefan's constant; T_f = Flame temperature

Differential Equations for the System

Manipulation of equations (1) and (11), given the auxiliary equations indicated and together with equation (12), enables three coupled ordinary differential equations to be derived in the general form:

$$dT/dt = F_1(T,Z,R) \tag{13}$$

$$dZ/dt = F_2(T,Z,R) \tag{14}$$

$$dR/dt = F_3(T,Z,R) \tag{15}$$

These equations define a system having the three state-variables T,Z and R. The functions F_1 and F_2 are given in Appendix 1; F_3 is indicated above.

INSTABILITY AND FLASHOVER

The differential equations (13)-(15) may be solved simultaneously in order to identify those conditions which give rise to instability. The concepts of nonlinear dynamics have been described briefly in reference [2]. In particular, the concept of eigenvalue has been employed in order to find the conditions which cause a system to lose stability. A system becomes unstable if the real part of an eigenvalue, λ, becomes positive. As the fire grows a radius may be reached at which the system becomes unstable. After that the fire would be expected to increase rapidly. If there is sufficient fuel, i.e., the maximum radius is large enough, to allow a ventilation-controlled (VC) fire to exist then that is the state which would be expected to result. For a domestic-sized room, of typical contents and ventilation opening, that would correspond to a post-flashover fire. If there is insufficient fuel present to allow ventilation control then a serious fire may still result, even if the regime is still fuel-controlled (FC). The essential point is that, after instability has occurred, a rapid development to the maximum fuel area available or the maximum sustainable with VC, whichever occurs first, would be expected.

ILLUSTRATIVE SIMULATIONS

Calculations have been conducted for the case of a compartment 4m by 4m by 3m high with a ventilation opening from floor to ceiling of width 0.4m. (The opening factor equivalent to this vent is similar to that of a typical door.) The fuel is taken to be polyurethane foam. Details of the input are given in Appendix 2. Results for the case where the maximum fire radius, R_m, is 0.6m are illustrated in Figure 2(a)-(d). These graphs show variation with time of: (a) Upper layer temperature, T; (b) Upper layer depth, Z; (c) Fire radius, R, and (d) λ, the least negative eigenvalue. It is found that the system becomes unstable at a critical value of the radius, R_c, equal to 0.34m. This is the point at which the relevant transient eigenvalue goes positive. After that the radius increases rapidly to its maximum value accompanied by a sharp rise in T and Z and resulting in a VC fire. A phase plane diagram illustrating dependence upon initial conditions of T and Z is shown in Figure 3. The trajectories show developments with time and increasing radius. That is, radius is a third dimension perpendicular to the plane; the trajectories do not overlap. All trajectories go to the final, VC, state.

If the maximum radius is greater than the critical radius but not large enough to allow ventilation-control then a fuel-controlled state will result. In such a case the temperature reached may still be very serious in relation to life safety or property loss, even though the regime is still FC. The phase plane diagram for such a case, with Rm = 0.5m, is shown in Figure 4. It is seen that there are two possible final states depending upon the initial conditions. (In order to compare with the results of the model of reference [1] for a room of the same dimensions and fuel, the equivalent input to that used in [1] has also been used. This produces a value for Rc of 0.27m, which may be compared with Rc = 0.42m for the model of reference [1].)

CONCLUSION

A nonlinear model has been developed within a zonal formulation which has the state-variables: upper layer temperature, T; upper layer depth, Z and fire radius, R. It has been shown that, for a given set of input parameters, a fire radius is reached at which the system becomes unstable. This point of instability is associated with an eigenvalue becoming positive. After the critical radius has been reached, a rapid development to the maximum fuel radius available would be expected, given sufficient ventilation. If the maximum radius of the fuel is not sufficient to allow ventilation-control then a fuel-controlled state will be

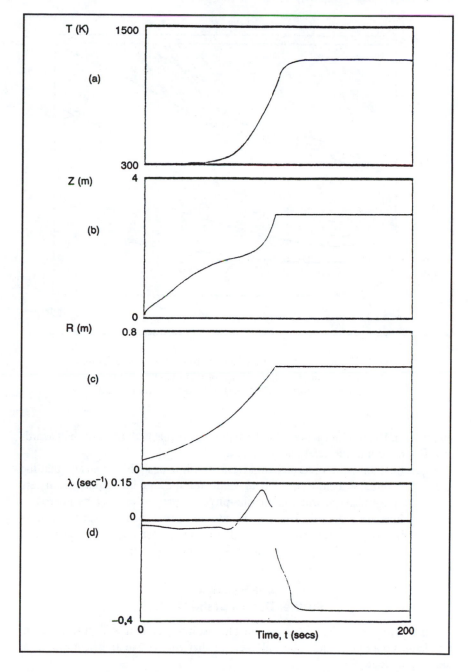

Figure 2. Results for the case with $R_m = 0.6$ meters; (a) upper layer temperature, T; (b) upper layer depth, Z; (c) fire radius, R; (d) transient eigenvalue, λ.

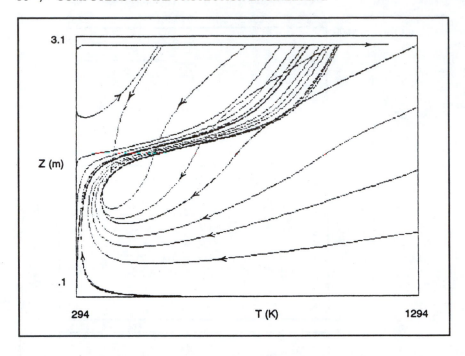

Figure 3. Phase plane diagram for the case with R_m = 0.6 meters;
(Z: upper layer depth; T: upper layer temperature.
The axis for radius, R, is perpendicular to the plane.)

maintained. Even with fuel-control the temperature reached may still be hazardous with respect to life safety or property loss.

In practical terms, in order to avoid flashover, it is desirable to ensure that the fire radius remains below the critical value for the system. Input parameters corresponding to geometrical or thermo-physical properties may be altered in order to increase the critical radius. In addition protection measures, such as sprinklers, may be used to try to ensure that the critical radius is not reached. In such a way this model may assist in the assessment of a design.

APPENDIX 1
Further Details of the Model

Net heat flux to the fuel, $\dot{q}''$; is assumed to result from radiative heat fluxes from the flame, upper layer and upper surface, together with convective heat flux from the flaming region;

$$\dot{q}'' = \varepsilon_b \, \varepsilon_{fb} \, \sigma \, (T_f 4 - T_b 4) + h_{cl} \, (T_f - T_b) + \varepsilon_l \, \varepsilon_b \, \phi \, \sigma \, T^4$$
$$+ \, \phi_{usb} \, \varepsilon_{us} \, (1 - \varepsilon_l) \, \varepsilon_b \sigma T_{us} 4 \tag{A1}$$

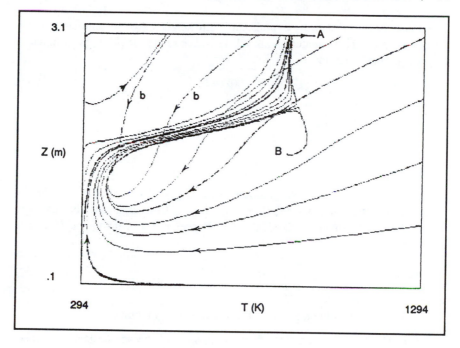

Figure 4. Phase plane diagram for the case with $R_m = 0.5$ meters.
All trajectories go to the point A except those indicated as b which go to point B.
(Z: upper layer depth; T: upper layer temperature. The axis for radius, R,
is perpendicular to the plane.)

where:

ε_b = Emissivity of the surface at the fire base; ε_{fb} = Emissivity of the flame to the fire base; T_b = Temperature of the surface at the fire base; h_{cl} = Convective heat transfer coefficient from the flame to the fire base; ε_l = Emissivity of the smoke layer;

ϕ = Configuration factor from the underside of the smoke layer to the fire base; ϕ_{usb} = Configuration factor from the upper surface to the fire base; ε_{us} = Emissivity of the upper surface

The emissivity from the flame to the fire base has been assumed to be given by [7] the equation:

$$\varepsilon_{fb} = 1 - \exp(-K_{fb} L_{fb}) \tag{A2}$$

where:

K_{fb} = Extinction coefficient of the flame
L_{fb} = Mean beam length to the base of the flame

The flame is assumed to be cylindrical, with height equal to diameter, which allows L_{fb} to be approximated as $L_{fb} = 1.42\ R$; see reference [8]. ε_1 is assumed to be given by the equation:

$$\varepsilon_1 = 1 - \exp\left(- K_f\ L_l\right) \tag{A3}$$

where:

K_f = Extinction coefficient for the layer
L_l = Mean beam length through the layer; see [9]

$$= 1.8\ L_1\ L_2\ Z\ /\ (L_1\ L_2 + L_1\ Z + L_2\ Z) \tag{A4}$$

L_1 = Compartment length; L_2 = Compartment width

Density of the upper layer, ρ; is assumed to be given by equation (A5) below whilst the interface is above the floor. This results from assuming that pressure within the compartment is fixed at ambient pressure and using the ideal gas equation:

$$\rho = \rho_a\ T_a\ /\ T \tag{A5}$$

where:

ρ_a = Density of ambient air; T_a = Temperature of ambient air

If the interface reaches the floor then the density of the smoke layer is subsequently assumed to be a constant fraction, DENC, of the ambient density.

Rate of energy input to the upper layer from the fire, $\dot{Q}_1$; assumed to be a constant fraction, N_1, of the heat release rate:

$$\dot{Q}_i = N_1\ \dot{Q}_f \tag{A6}$$

Enthalpy flow rate into the plume, $\dot{H}_i$; assumed to be given by:

$$\dot{H}_i = C_p\ \dot{m}_e\ T_a + C_p\ \dot{m}_f\ T_f \tag{A7}$$

where:

C_p = Specific heat at constant pressure of ambient air

The specific heat at constant pressure of the volatiles is assumed to be C_p. The flow rate of entrained gases, $\dot{m}_e$, is assumed to be given by:

$$\dot{m}_e = \dot{m}_p\ \text{EXFUN} + \dot{m}_v\ (1 - \text{EXFUN}) \tag{A8}$$

where:

$\dot{m}_p$ = Plume mass flow rate, taken from Zukoski [4].

$$= 0.076\ (\dot{Q}_i)^{1/3}\ (Z_1)^{5/3} \tag{A9}$$

Z_1 = Height of layer base above virtual source

$$= Z_0 + Z_2$$

Z_0 = Height of fuel surface above virtual source
Z_2 = Height of layer base above fuel surface

The expression for the position of the virtual source has been taken from Heskestad [10]:

$$Z_0 = 2.04 \, R - 0.083 \, (\dot{Q}_i)^{2/5} \tag{A10}$$

$\dot{m}_v$ = Vent inflow rate, from Prahl and Emmons [5]

$$= (2/3) \, C_d \, A_v \, \rho_a \, \{2 \, g \, H(1-[\rho/\rho_a])(N-D)\}^{1/2}\{N + [D/2]\} \tag{A11}$$

where:
$N = H_n/H$; $D = (H - Z)/H$; g = Acceleration due to gravity;
A_v = Vent area; H_n = Height of the neutral plane

The minimum height of the neutral plane, H_{nmin} is assumed to be a fixed ratio, H_{nrat}, of the vent height, i.e., $H_{nmin} = H_{nrat} \, H$
The function EXFUN has been used to switch from the plume equation to the vent flow equation and has been assumed to be given by:

$$
\begin{aligned}
\text{EXFUN} &= 0 & &\text{if } Z = H \\
&= 1 & &\text{if } Z < (H-H_n) \\
&= \exp\{\text{Conex}[(H-Z-H_n)/(H-Z)]\} & &\text{if } (H-H_n) < Z < H \\
\text{Conex} &= \text{A dimensionless constant} & &
\end{aligned}
\tag{A12}
$$

Temperature of the upper surface, T_{us}; is derived by assuming the heat transferred from the upper layer to the upper surface is equal to heat conducted through the upper surface. The rate of heat conduction through the upper surface is assumed to be given by:

$$\dot{Q}_{cond} = A_{us} \, D_c \, (T_{us} - T_a) \tag{A13}$$

where:
A_{us} = Area of the upper surface; D_c = Effective conductive coefficient.

The rate of heat transfer from the upper layer to the upper surface, Q_{ous}, is assumed to be given by:

$$\dot{Q}_{ous} = A_{us} \, \{ \, \epsilon_l \, \epsilon_{us} \, \sigma \, (T^4 - T_{us}4) + h_{c2} \, (T - T_{us}) \tag{A14}$$

where:
h_{c2} = Convective heat transfer coefficient from the upper layer to upper surface.

Equating the right hand sides of equations (A14) and (A15) produces a quartic in T_{us}. This quartic is solved numerically as part of the calculation.
Rate of energy loss from upper layer, other than via smoke flow, $\dot{Q}_o$; assumed to be given by radiative loss from the lower surface of the smoke layer to the lower

surface of the compartment and out of the vent, together with radiative and convective losses to the upper surface:

$$\dot{Q}_o = A_f \, \phi \, \varepsilon_1 \, \varepsilon_b \, \sigma \, T^4 + (A_{ls} - A_f) \, \sigma \, \varepsilon_{ls} \, \varepsilon_1 \, (T^4 - T_a4) + \dot{Q}_{ous} \qquad \text{(A15)}$$

where:

A_{ls} = Area of lower surface; ε_{ls} = Emissivity of lower surface

Enthalpy flow rate from smoke layer out of vent, $\dot{H}_o$; assumed to be:

$$\dot{H}_o = C_p \, \dot{m}_o \, T \qquad \text{(A16)}$$

The mass flow rate out, $\dot{m}_o$, is taken from Rockett [3]:

$$\dot{m}_o = (2/3) \, C_d \, A_v \, \rho_a \{ 1 - (Hn/H) \}^{3/2} \, \{ 2 \, g \, H(T_a/T)(1 - [T_a/T]) \}^{1/2} \qquad \text{(A17)}$$

During the earlier stages of a fire the neutral plane is assumed to be at the level of the interface. If the interface reaches the floor then m_o is subsequently assumed to be given by:

$$\dot{m}_o = \dot{m}_v + \dot{m}_f \qquad \text{(A18)}$$

The functions F_1 *and* F_2; F_1 is derived in reference [2] and corresponds to equation (19) there. F_2 is derived from equation (5) and is given by:

$$F_2 = \{ \, Z \, F_1 \, / \, T \, \} + \{ (T \, / \, [A \, \rho_a \, T_a])(\dot{m}_e + \dot{m}_f - \dot{m}_o) \} \qquad \text{(A19)}$$

If the interface reaches the floor then Z is assumed to be constant at H. That is, F_2 becomes zero in that case.

Maximum heat release rate, $\dot{Q}_{fmax}$; see [7]; assumed to be given by:

$$\dot{Q}_{fmax} = 1500 \, A_v \, (H)^{1/2} \, kW \qquad \text{(A20)}$$

APPENDIX 2
Input Data

C_d: 0.68 ; see reference [5]. C_p: 1.04 kJ/kg ; see reference [7].
Conex: 3 ; found by experience to give a plausible change over.
DENC: 0.5 ; mean value between 0 and 1 assumed.
D_c: 0.004543 kW/m^{2}K ; assumed = k/δ where k = thermal conductivity and δ = wall thickness (k: 0.0001154 kW/mK ; Marinite XL assumed, see [11]. δ: 0.0254m)

h_{c1}: 0.02 kW/m^{2}K ; the convective heat transfer coefficient for free convection has been stated as ranging typically from 0.005 to 0.025 kW/m^{2}K, see [7]. As the flaming volume is at a relatively high temperature a higher value within this range has been assumed.

h_{c2}: 0.01 kW/m^{2}K ; a typical value, see [12]. H: 3metres

H_v: 2190 kJ/kg, see reference [11]. H_c: 2.87(10^4) kJ/kg, see [11].

H_{nrat}: 0.45, see e.g. reference [13]. K_f, K_{fb}: both 1.3 m^{-1}; see [11].

L_1: 4metres. L_2: 4metres. L_3: 3metres. N_1: 0.7 ; see e.g. [14]. S_r: 9.78

T_a: 293 K. T_b: 600 K; see e.g. [11]. T_f: 1400 K; see e.g [7]. W: 0.4metres.

ε_b: 1. ε_{ls}: 0.5. ε_{us}: 0.5. ϕ: 0.95. ϕ_{usb}: 0.95. χ: 1.

ρ_a: 1.1 kg/m^3; see reference [7].

REFERENCES

1. A. N. Beard, D. D. Drysdale, P. G. Holborn, and S. R. Bishop, A Non-Linear Model of Flashover, *Fire Science & Technology, 12*, pp. 11-27, 1992.
2. S. R. Bishop, P. G. Holborn, A. N. Beard, and D. D. Drysdale, Nonlinear Dynamics of Flashover in Compartment Fires, *Fire Safety Journal, 21*, pp. 11-45, 1993.
3. J. A. Rockett, Fire Induced Gas Flow in an Enclosure, *Combustion Science & Technology, 12*, pp. 165-175, 1976.
4. E. E. Zukoski, T. Kubota, and E. Cetegen, Entrainment in Fire Plumes, *Fire Safety Journal, 3*, pp. 107-121, 1980/81.
5. J. Prahl and H. W. Emmons, Fire Induced Flow through an Opening, *Combustion and Flame, 25*, pp. 369-385, 1975.
6. H. W. Emmons, The Calculation of a Fire in a Large Building, *Journal of Heat Transfer, 105*, pp. 151-158, 1983.
7. D. D. Drysdale, *Introduction to Fire Dynamics*, Wiley, Chichester, 1985.
8. C. L. Tien, K. Y. Lee, and A. J. Stretton, Radiation Heat Transfer, *SFPE Handbook of Fire Protection Engineering*, pp. 1-92 to 1-106; Society of Fire Protection Engineers, Boston, 1988.
9. J. De Ris, Fire Radiation—A Review, *17th Symposium (International) on Combustion*, pp. 1003-1016, The Combustion Institute, Pittsburgh, 1979.
10. G. Heskestad, Virtual Origins of Fire Plumes, *Fire Safety Journal, 5*, pp. 109-114, 1983.
11. R. L. Alpert, Influence of Enclosures on Fire Growth: Vol. 1; Test Data, Test 7, Report No. OAOR2, Factory Mutual Research Corporation, Norwood, New Jersey, 1977.
12. G. T. Atkinson and D. D. Drysdale, Convective Heat Transfer from Fire Gases, *Fire Safety Journal, 19*, pp. 217-245, 1992.
13. V. Babrauskas and B. Williamson, Post-Flashover Compartment Fires: Basis of a Theoretical Model, *Fire & Materials, 2*, pp. 39-53, 1978.
14. G. Heskestad, Engineering Relations for Fire Plumes, *Fire Safety Journal, 7*, pp. 25-32, 1984.

CHAPTER 5

Causal Probabilistic Networks with Learning: A Diagnosis Decisional Tool

F. Casciati and L. Faravelli

This chapter provides a framework in which the operative conditions of existing buildings can be assessed on a probabilistic basis. The decision maker system is able to learn from the expertise it collects during its service. The supporting mathematical tool makes use of a causal probabilistic network (CPN) to represent the knowledge domain.

A diagnostic problem requires the identification of the most likely diagnosis and specification of the motivations leading to it. The problem is generally approached by procedures, working under uncertainty, which are developed by experts as a sequence of abductive, deductive, and inductive steps.

A simplification is achieved by regarding the diagnostic problem as the iden-tification of the actual state of a system on the basis of the result of its observable aspects. This is a classification problem and classification techniques can be adopted to solve it.

To classify an object on the basis of one of its characteristics is to identify the class to which the object belongs: the class must be selected, within a finite number, on the basis of the available measures. A classification rule is a sys-tematic rule which assigns objects to a class. Let X and Y be the vector of the measurements over the observable variables and the vector which determines the class, respectively. Let X be the outcome space for vector X. Moreover, without loss of generality, let the vector Y be simplified into the scalar discrete variable Y, with K different values: the space $\mathcal{Y}$ results $(1, ..., k, ..., K)$.

The introduction of a classification rule is the introduction of the mapping $\mathcal{F}$.

$$\mathcal{F}: X \times \mathcal{Y} \rightarrow [0,1] \tag{1}$$

which, for any realization $\underline{X}$ of X leads one to the decisional rule:

$$d(\underline{X}) = j \quad \text{if} \quad \mathcal{F}(\underline{X},j) = \max_{k \in \Psi} \mathcal{F}(\underline{X},k) \tag{2}$$

The classification techniques can be grouped, according to the nature of the mapping $\mathcal{F}$, into:

- *symbolic techniques* aiming at the identification of the Boolean function $\mathcal{F}$ which, for each couple (X,Y) in $X \times Y$, assumes the value 1 or 0 provided that Y is, or is not, respectively, the true class for X. The following relation holds:

$$\sum_{j=1}^{K} \mathcal{F}(\underline{X}, Y = j) = 1 \quad \supset \underline{X} \in X \tag{3}$$

- *probabilistic techniques* aiming at the identification of a function $\mathcal{F}$ which, for each couple (X,Y) in $X \times Y$ assumes a value in [0,1], giving the probability that Y be the true class for X. The following relation holds:

$$\sum_{j=1}^{K} \mathcal{F}(\underline{X}, Y = j) = 1 \quad \supset \underline{X} \in X \tag{4}$$

The function $\mathcal{F}$ can be regarded as the conditional probability Prob[Y | X]. The results of symbolic techniques can also be read as the certainty result of a probabilistic technique, but the first ones do not give the couple (X,Y) a random nature.

A classification rule also represents a rule of partition of the space X into subsets X_j such that:

$$X_j = \{\underline{X} : d(\underline{X}) = j\} \quad j = 1, ..., K \tag{5}$$

with

$$\bigcup_{j}^{K} X_j = X \quad X_i \cap X_j = 0 \tag{6}$$

Each of these subsets is characterized by the circumstance that all the vectors X in it present the same value of the variable Y.

From an operative point of view one distinguishes:

1. *parametric approaches* aiming at the identification of the function $\mathcal{F}$, provided a model (or a class of models) depending on r unknown parameters. The method becomes *unbearable*, from a computational point of view, for a high dimension of the space X or for a large number of classes of Y.

2. *non parametric approaches* aiming at the identification of the partition of X, without introducing any model for the function $\mathcal{F}$. The approximation error depends on the dishomogeneity of the response Y over the partition subsets.

To build a classification rule needs the availability of a set of data with known classification. This information forms a *training set* (or a *learning sample*) of size N:

$$\mathcal{W} = (\underline{X}_i \underline{Y}_i); \, i = 1, ..., N\} \tag{7}$$

The single realization in $\mathcal{W}$ is independent of and comparable with each other. The learning sample can be used in different ways:

- a *sequential approach* updates the classification system case by case;
- a *batch approach* determines the classification structure, but its update requires that a new learning sample, of enlarged size, be considered;
- a *mixed approach* starts as a batch approach, but, as new cases arrive, a sequential learning is adopted.

A decision rule result in a simple description of the training data. Its predictive use preliminarily requires the incorporation of the appropriate degree of generalization. Unfortunately, description and prediction are conflicting characteristics and the correct equilibrium should be achieved for an optimization of the results.

Four main techniques are developed in the literature for the solution of a classification problem [1]:

1. **machine learning techniques**; they include [2]:
   - *learning from examples* which is a process of generalization from examples;
   - *learning by analogy* which transfers to new problems the information achieved in already solved problems, of different physical meaning, but governed by the same basic relations;
   - *learning by discovery* which tries to identify the regularities in the problem under investigation and to understand them.
   - *learning by causal analysis* which leads one to build the correct model on the basis of the experienced solution failures.
2. **neural networks**; the name denotes a technology by which computers learn directly from data. For the basic back-propagation algorithm, a network is formed by at least three layers of nodes with links between two subsequent layers. The input layer is passive: it receives the values X as input and, hence, the number of its nodes equates to the size of vector X. The other layers actively process the data. Each node of the output layer produces a single element of the response vector Y. The hidden layers have not a direct relation with input and output, but their presence permits one to model complex nonlinear functions.

After training with the sample $\mathcal{W}$, a check with a different set of data $\mathcal{W}'$, with $\mathcal{W} \cap \mathcal{W}' = 0$ should be pursued (validation) as a measure of the reliability of the trained network: even well trained networks, in fact, can prove inadequate.

After training and validation, the data presented at the input layer will produce values at the output layer: the network acts as a model mapping input data into output values, according to the teaching of the training sample $\mathcal{W}$.

3. **standard statistical techniques**; for a discrete variable, the appropriate generalized linear models are the so-called multinomial logistic models. They assume a multinomial probability distribution for the response variable. Let $\underline{X}_i$ be the vector of the input variables and $\underline{Y}_i$ the response variables with K classes, one writes:

$$\underline{Y}_i \sim \mathcal{M}(p_k) \qquad i = 1, ..., N \tag{8}$$

with the probability as function of the input variables:

$$p_k = p_k(\underline{X}_i) \tag{9}$$

To build a predictive classification system means, therefore, to identify the best model by which one estimates the probability associated with each class of the response variable. In a diagnostic problem, however, handling more than three or four input variables may prove difficult.

4. **expert systems**: they simulate the knowledge of an expert in a specific domain. The main problem to be solved is the uncertainty treatment, which can be approached in three different ways: logistic (or non numerical), *ad hoc* and numerical. The latter relies on probability theory, on fuzzy set theory or on theory of evidence [3].

Within the probabilistic approach, one assumes each piece of information be represented by a discrete variable defined over a probability space [4, 5]. The problem is therefore governed by a joint probability defined over all the possible combinations of classes of the variables. It is the result of relations among variables as provided by experts. This knowledge can be expressed by rules of the type *if-then* or by causal links. The latter way provides a qualitative structure on which the joint probability can be built: the operative tool of the approach is graph theory and the result is a causal probabilistic network (CPN) [6, 7].

The main advantage of a CPN model is its capability of exploiting and incorporating the physical understanding of the phenomenon under investigation.

The efficiency of the previous techniques should be evaluated in terms of three components:

- *practicability* is the availability of the correct hardware for the developer of the predictive system; it becomes a straightforward adoption of the resulting device if the problem is regarded from the user point of view. All the procedures listed previously are operative under systems such as DOS or Unix and, hence, require, as hardware, personal computers or workstations of common use in engineering;

- *adequacy* is the capability of explaining results and compatibility with stand-ard technical approaches. Neural networks are quite unsatisfactory, under this aspect, due to their black-box nature. The other three techniques offer good explanation characteristics; the graphical features of classification trees and causal networks show limits which are quite compatible with the complexity of engineering problems;

- *capability of learning* is the possibility of a sequential update of the predic-tive structure as new cases with known classifications are made available. For neural networks this property is a natural feature, but it is not implemented in machine-learning and statistical techniques. By contrast, a sequential update has been made operative for causal probabilistic networks a couple of years ago [8].

The previous screening of available classification techniques shows the suitability of using causal probabilistic networks as classification schemes: they will be illustrated in the next section. The implementation in a computer code, a learning extension and the development of a numerical example are the topics of the remaining three sections.

2. CAUSAL PROBABILISTIC NETWORKS

The common use of causal probabilistic networks covers the automatic learning from clinical databases. Several aspects of the engineering profession, however, are today requiring a preliminary diagnosis showing the reasons for taking an action and the best way for doing it [9-11].

As previous applications, databases of seismic vulnerability of existing masonry buildings have been created [12] and exploited in expert systems [3, 13]. Causal networks have also been proposed as a good tool for structural safety diagnosis [6, 14].

2.1 Definitions

A Bayesian network is defined by an acyclic graph $G^{\rightarrow} = (\mathcal{V}, \mathcal{E}^{\rightarrow})$ (where the apex $\rightarrow$ denotes the oriented nature of graph and links) and by a set of conditional probability distributions $p(\upsilon|pa(\upsilon))$, $\supset \upsilon \in \mathcal{V}$: $pa(\upsilon)$ denotes the parents of υ, i.e., the nodes from which oriented links start toward υ. Such a structure is suitable for representing a *set of events*, the graph vertices, and a set of causal relations, the oriented connections. The network topology is the qualitative component of the model; the probability distributions provide the dependency in a quantitative way.

Assume such a static representation be assigned. One can try to use it in a dynamic process by which the status of uncertain knowledge is updated on the basis of the collection of new data. The probabilities associated with variables for which a direct observation is still lacking should be modified as new pieces of evidence arrive. This means to compute from the joint distribution

$$p(\mathcal{V}) = \prod_{\upsilon \varepsilon v} p(\upsilon|\text{pa}(\upsilon)) \qquad (10)$$

the conditional distributions provided that a set of observed values become available,

$$\text{Prob}(Q = q|Z = z), \text{ with } Q, Z \subset \mathcal{V} \qquad (11)$$

(and Q may also represent a single element). In the following each node is characterized by a (discrete) random variable with a finite number of states.

The decomposition of the joint distribution, by which the computations required by equation (11) can be conducted in an efficient way, has the form:

$$p(\mathcal{V}) = \frac{\prod_{i=1}^{k} pci\,(C_i)}{\prod_{i=2}^{k} psi\,(S_i)} \qquad (12)$$

with C_i denoting the i-th *clique* [15] and S_i the i-th *separation set*. To explain this point, assume the original network be transformed in a moral graph by adding links between unlinked parent nodes (*unmarried*) and by removing the link orientation. Moreover, let the result be triangulated. In the original set of nodes $\mathcal{V}$, it is possible to identify complete subsets of nodes, Ci, called *cliques*, so that each *clique* is the maximum group of nodes each linked with each other. These *cliques* are then ordered in the *junction tree* in such a way that if two of them, C_i and Cj, have common elements, a link is introduced between them. The common elements form the separation set S_i. This property guarantees that any new information, concerning an individual node, which enters the network, be propagated in a consistent and non redundant way.

The problem is now to move from the representation of equation (10) to that of equation (12).

The basic theoretical statement for the procedure is: If a recursive factorization with respect to $G^{\rightarrow}$ exists for a probabilistic model, it can also be factorized with respect to the moral graph G^m and, hence, preserves the same Markov properties with respect to this moral graph [15]. The resulting procedure consists of the following two steps:

1. The oriented graph $G^{\rightarrow}$ is transformed into the moral graph G^m. If the latter one is not triangulated, links are added so that all the cycles ≥ 4 are interrupted.
2. The algorithm of *maximum cardinality search* provides a node order associated, in a unique way, to a perfect clique order $\{C_1, ... C_l\}$.

The previous steps provide the topology required by the decomposition rule in equation (12); but the quantitative assessment of the marginal distributions in equation (12) requires further steps. One imposes the moral (triangulated) graph G^m to have the same dependency structure of the initial network $G^{\rightarrow}$; the latter one, in fact, except for the orientation, is contained in G^m. For this purpose the factors in equation (10) are grouped so that the resulting functions are defined over subsets of variables in a single clique. The algorithm can be summarized as follows:

$$\begin{aligned}
&\textit{initialization} \quad \psi(C_i) = 1, \supset i \in \{1, ..., k\} \\
&\textit{step j-th} \quad \text{let } i \text{ be such that } \{v_j\} \cup \text{pa}(v_j) \subseteq C_i: \\
&\qquad\qquad \psi(C_i) \leftarrow \psi(C_i) \times p(v_j|\text{pa}(v_j))
\end{aligned} \tag{13}$$

where ψ denotes potential functions. In this way each factor $p(v_j|\text{pa}(v_j))$ is assigned once, even if $\{v_j\} \cup \text{pa}(v_j)$ is contained in more than one clique. (The operator $\times$ by which the functions $\psi(C_i)$ are built is the standard product: nevertheless one multiplies functions defined over different sets and, hence, the definition of product must be extended.) When each $p(v_j|\text{pa}(v_i))$ has been assigned to a single $\psi(\cdot)$, some functions $\psi(\cdot)$ may remain at their initial value, i.e., 1. This certainly occurs if additional links were introduced.

As a result, one obtains a product of potential functions $\psi(\cdot)$ over the cliques of G^m; such a product is assumed, except for a normalization constant, to be the joint distribution:

$$p(\mathcal{V}) \propto \prod_{i=1}^{k} \psi(C_i) \tag{14}$$

and equation (12) can be written in the form (14) by defining the functions $\psi(\cdot)$ over the separation sets equal to 1. (Of course in equation (12) a zero denominator means a zero value for the l.h.s.)

Since the potential functions were derived separately one from each other, a separate normalization would not be appropriate for deriving a probability distribution. In this way, in fact, there is no guarantee that a subsequent marginalization over elements common to more than one clique would produce the same result.

By contrast, conditions of global equilibrium must be imposed to the potential:

$$\sum_{C_i \backslash C_j} \psi_{C_i}(C_i) \propto \sum_{C_j \backslash C_i} \psi_{C_j}(C_j), \quad \supset i \neq j, \text{ such that } C_i \cap C_j \neq 0 \qquad (15)$$

where C_i/C_j denotes the complement to C_j of C_i. The operation leading to the global equilibrium (15) is called *calibration of the joint tree*.

2.2 Computation Algorithm

The propagation algorithm proceeds by modifying the single potential functions in a sequence of steps during which equation (12) is always satisfied. At the end the potentials will contain the new information and will express the marginal probability mass functions of the corresponding set of variables. From the marginal distributions of the cliques it is then straightforward to obtain the mass probability functions of each node.

The basic operation for achieving the local equilibrium, i.e., the equilibrium between two adjacent nodes, is called *absorption*. To say that clique C_i absorbs from C_j means to consider the following transformations:

$$\psi'(C_i) \leftarrow \frac{\psi(C_i)}{\sum_{\rho_i} \psi(C_i)} \times \sum_{\rho_j} \psi(C_j)$$

with $\rho_i = C_i \setminus S, \rho_j = C_j \setminus S, S = C_i \cap C_j$, where $C_i \backslash S$ denotes the complement to S of C_i, and

$$\psi'(S) \leftarrow \sum_{\rho_j} \psi(C_j)$$

The potentials $\psi(C_i)$ and $\psi(C_j)$ are now in equilibrium because

$$\sum_{\rho_i} \psi'(C_i) = \sum_{\rho_i} \frac{\psi(C_i)}{\sum_{\rho_i} \psi(C_i)} \sum_{\rho_j} \psi(C_j) = \sum_{\rho_j} \psi(C_j).$$

Every time the potential of a clique is modified due to absorption, in order to reach the equilibrium, it is necessary to transmit the effects to all the cliques, adjacent but different from the ones from which the absorption occurred. The process, then, proceeds till the terminal nodes are reached. At each step, each clique interacts with the adjacent ones and the separation sets identify the elements involved.

After $\psi(C_i)$ is set as in equation (15) and $\psi(S_i) \equiv 1$, the successive operation sequence can be summarized as follows:

- *information collection*: starting from any clique, C_i, one *addresses* toward C_i the information coming from all the other nodes. This means that the potential of C_i *absorbs* from all the adjacent nodes, which have already absorbed from the adjacent ones (except C_i). The absorption proceeds till the terminal nodes are reached. The clique C_i is no longer in equilibrium with the adjacent ones: the next step will represent it;

- *information distribution*: from C_i information is propagated through all the tree, following an inverse path: the adjacent cliques absorb from C_i and this starts a chain of analogous absorptions from the potentials of adjacent cliques, till all the tree branches are visited.

These two stages achieve a global consistency: the marginal distribution of each variable (i.e., of each node of the original causal network) can then be derived from any potential function having that variable as argument.

In summary, one builds, from the original causal network, a joint tree (i.e., the clique tree) having the same probabilistic model of the network (equation (10)). This tree is then used as a *calculator* using the decomposition in equation (12). This avoids the direct computation of the joint probability distribution and all the marginal distributions can be derived by simple transformations of the potential functions. Each operation has just a local character in the joint tree topology, since each clique only interacts with the adjacent ones.

2.2 Evidence Propagation

Assume now that one has new pieces of evidence (on some subsets of variables) and wishes to update the marginal distributions. It is necessary to compute conditional probability of the type (11). For the sake of simplicity, let $Q \cup Z$ be equal to $\mathcal{V}$. Since

$$p(Q|Z = z) = p(Q,z)/p(z) \propto p(Q,z) \tag{16}$$

the computation only consists in a normalization of the expression obtained from the joint distribution after substitution of the observed values in Z. This operation can be conducted by the same initial calibration process which makes the joint tree globally consistent.

Again the procedure works along the joint tree topology in such a way that each clique only interacts with the adjacent ones. It can be regarded as an information flow between *objects*, the cliques, which communicate through specific *links*, the separation tests. Its implementation in an object programming environment, therefore, seems to be especially attractive [16]: its guidelines are sketched in the next section.

3. ALGORITHM IMPLEMENTATION

The algorithm of the previous section has been implemented in the working environment *Nexpert* [13]. A comparison with the public domain code BAIES [17] is also developed.

3.1 An Object-Oriented Approach

The object-oriented approach is adopted for the development of the required numerical computations as well as for data representation and for the preliminary operations by which the causal network is transformed into a joint tree.

The working environment *Nexpert Object* [18] has been selected for this purpose due to its particular flexibility in representing the data structure and the calculation rules. The data are represented through *objects* (elementary items) and *classes* (object collections). For both of them it is possible to define *attributes* (or *slots*, i.e., properties having a numerical, alphanumerical or logical character) which can also be specified by procedures (*metaslots*).

The inferential model is made by general rules of the type

IF ... (*Left Hand Side*) THEN *hypothesis* AND DO ... (*Right Hand Side*).

Moreover, each rule is associated with a Boolean variable (*hypothesis*) which can be used within any other rule.

The classes were defined as follows:

- TABLES, whose objects are the initial condition distributions table_i; the attributes are: child, name of the node (variable); parent_j, name of the variables which are *causes* of child; clique, number (*rank*) of the clique to which the table must be attributed for the potential calculus;

- NODES, with the single nodes of the causal network described by *slots*: label, name of the node; node_id, initial order number; node_rank, order number assigned by the *maximum cardinality search*; size, work variable;

- CLIQUES, whose objects are the cliques obtained by the transformation of the initial network; the following attributes are defined: clique_rank, *rank* assigned after the node ordering; collect, flag for the activation of the procedure of information collection; distribute, flag for the activation of the procedure of information distribution; parent, *rank* of the parent clique.

Object programming has been used to solve, in particular, the graph transformation and the information propagation along the joint tree [15, 16, 19].

By coupling the techniques of object programming available in *Nexpert* with subroutines in *C language* for the calibration calculation, a complete system of causal network modeling, and, hence, of probabilistic expert systems, has been assembled. Its special feature is its capability to provide a graphical representation during the different steps of the analysis.

3.2 Existing Software

BAIES is an experimental computer code for the analysis of Bayesian networks of discrete variables [17]. It is a probabilistic expert system for computing the marginal probabilities of oriented graphs whose nodes represent discrete random variables: the properties of conditional independence are captured in the topological structure of the acyclic oriented graphic. In it several methods of local propagation are implemented toward the updating of probabilities, or other quantities of interest which are characteristic of the single random variables, on the basis of new pieces of evidence.

The main characteristic of BAIES is its capabilities of learning from sets of incomplete data and of modifying, by Bayesian methods, the tables of conditional probabilities. The options of more common use provide:

- the joint tree of a given oriented graph;
- the marginal probabilities;
- the evidence propagation;
- the updating of the conditional probabilities, given a set of data, even incomplete, by the learning technique illustrated in the next section.

Unfortunately it does not present any graphical support.

4. LEARNING

Introduce an auxiliary node for each node; it represents a random quantity ϕ_v whose realizations specify the table of conditional probabilities:

$$p(\mathcal{V}, \phi) = \prod_{v \in V} p(v|pa(v), \phi_v)p(\phi_v) \qquad (17)$$

The additional variables ϕ_v can be formally regarded as a further parent of v. A priori they are assumed to be independent random variables, so that $p(\phi) = \prod_v p(\phi_v)$. The joint probability distribution is then:

$$p(\mathcal{V}) = \int p(\mathcal{V}, \phi)d\phi = \int \prod_v (v|pa(v), \phi_v)p(\phi_v)d\phi_v \qquad (18)$$

which is the expected value of the conditional probabilities for v. A further simplification can be introduced by assuming a local independence for separating ϕ_v into two components: they correspond to different configurations of pa(v), to be regarded as mutually independent random quantities. Figure 1 illustrates this possibility.

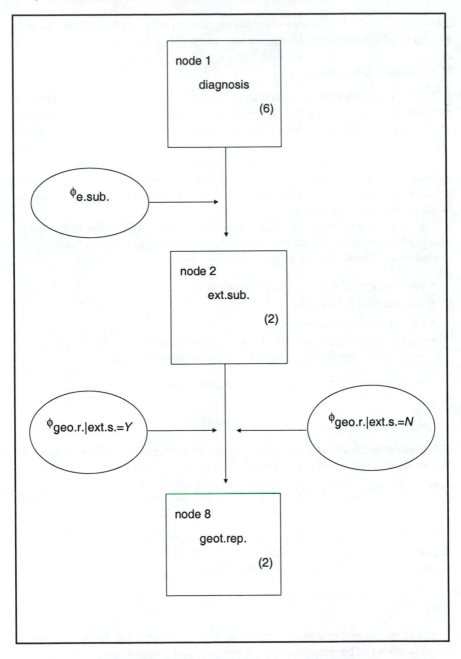

Figure 1. Detail from the network of Figure 2: the additional nodes represent the marginally independent random quantities ϕ_υ, $\upsilon \in \mathcal{V}$: their realizations specify the conditional probability table for the network.

The conditional probability tables are expressed in a parametric way by adopting a Dirichlet distribution: it becomes a *beta* distribution[1] for bivariate variables. Consider J random variables x_j, to $j = 1, ..., J$, independent and distributed according with a χ^2 distribution with $v_j > 0$, $j = 1, ..., J$ degrees of freedom. Build the random variables $y_j = \dfrac{x_j}{\sum_{l=0}^{J} x_l}$; then their joint probability density function is a Dirichlet distribution [20]:

$$p_{y_2,...,y_J}(y_2,...,y_J) = \frac{\Gamma\left(\frac{1}{2}\sum_{j=1}^{J} v_j\right)}{\prod_{j=1}^{J} \Gamma\left(\frac{1}{2}v_j\right)} \left[\prod_{j=2}^{J} y_j^{\left(\frac{1}{2}v_j - 1\right)}\right] \left(1 - \sum_{j=2}^{J} y_j\right)^{\left(\frac{1}{2}v_1 - 1\right)} \tag{19}$$

Put $\vartheta_j = \dfrac{1}{2} v_j$, equation (19) becomes the standard Dirichlet distribution $D[\vartheta_1, ..., \vartheta_J]$ of parameters $\vartheta_1, ..., \vartheta_J$:

$$p_{y_2,...,y_J}(y_2,...,y_J) = \frac{\Gamma\left(\sum_{j=1}^{J} \vartheta_j\right)}{\prod_{j=1}^{J} \Gamma(\vartheta_j)} \left[\prod_{j=2}^{J} y_j^{\left(\frac{1}{2}\vartheta_j - 1\right)}\right] \left(1 - \sum_{j=2}^{J} y_j\right)^{(\vartheta_1 - 1)} \tag{20}$$

with the constraints $y_j \geq 0$; $\sum_{j=2}^{J} y_j \leq 1$.

---

[1]The probability distribution *beta* characterizes a random variable whose values are limited over the interval (a,b). The probability density function is defined as

$$p_x(x) = \frac{1}{B(q,r)} \frac{(x-a)^{(q-1)}(b-x)^{(r-1)}}{(b-a)^{(q+r-1)}} \quad \begin{array}{l} a \leq x \leq b \\ \text{otherwise} \\ = \varnothing \end{array}$$

where q and r are parameters of the distribution and $B(q, r)$ is the *beta function*

$$B(q, r) = \int_0^1 x^{(q-1)} (1-x)^{(r-1)} \, dx = \frac{\Gamma(q)\Gamma(r)}{\Gamma(q+r)}$$

The corresponding mean μ_x and variance σ_x^2 are:

$$\mu_x = a + \frac{q}{q+r}(b-a)$$

$$\sigma_x^2 = \frac{qr}{(q+r)^2(q+r+1)}(b-a)^2$$

If $a = 0$ and $b = 1$ the relevant function is called a beta standard distribution.

With the additional position $\vartheta = \sum_{j=1}^{J} \vartheta_j$, y_j has a standard beta distribution of parameters ϑ_j e $\vartheta - \vartheta_j$, with mean and variance given by:

$$\mu_{y_j} = \frac{\vartheta_j}{\vartheta} \tag{21}$$

$$\sigma_{y_j}^2 = \frac{\vartheta_j(\vartheta - \vartheta_j)}{\vartheta^2(\vartheta + 1)} \tag{22}$$

Suppose that node υ be characterized by J states. Let the parent configuration $\overline{pa}(\upsilon)$ be assigned. One assumes that:

$$p(\upsilon|\overline{pa}(\upsilon),\phi_{\upsilon|pa(\upsilon)}) = \phi_{\upsilon}|p_{au}) \tag{23}$$

with the r.h.s. term distributed according to the Dirichlet distribution $\mathcal{D}[\vartheta_{\upsilon 1}, ...,\vartheta_{\upsilon J}]$. The parameters of this distribution represent a record of previous events and summarize the available experience. For the subsequent analysis the conditional probability used for the j-th class is from equation (18):

$$p(\upsilon_j|\overline{pa}(\upsilon)) = \frac{\vartheta_{\upsilon j}}{\vartheta_{\upsilon}} \tag{24}$$

4.1 Batch Learning

Batch learning is useful for the system initialization: the conditional probabilities are obtained as a combination of a priori information and available data. As new data arrives, one proceeds with the sequential learning of the next subsection.

Assume the results of N experiments are available; for the i-th of them let e_i be the observed evidence. The EM algorithm proceeds iteratively through two steps M and E:

step M:

$$p(\upsilon_j|\overline{pa}(\upsilon)) = \frac{\Lambda(\upsilon_j,\overline{pa})}{\Lambda(\overline{pa})} \tag{25}$$

where Λ denotes the number of observations expected from the marginal tables; step E: the number of expected observations is obtained from:

$$\Lambda(\overline{pa}) = \sum_{i=1}^{N} p(\overline{pa}(\upsilon)|e_i) \tag{26}$$

In the presence of experiments with missing data it is suitable to exploit the a priori information and to penalize the likelihood of the deviations from the a priori estimate. Step M can be substituted with:

step M':

$$p(\upsilon_j | \overline{pa}(\upsilon)) = \frac{\Lambda(\upsilon_j, \overline{pa}(\upsilon)) + \vartheta_{\upsilon j}}{\Lambda(\overline{pa}) + \vartheta} \qquad (27)$$

4.2 Sequential Learning

Assume now that evidence is collected one experiment at the time: each time the values ϕ_υ must be updated. One distinguishes two cases:

1. Let υ be observed in its j-th state, among the J possible ones, with pa(υ) = $\overline{pa}(\upsilon)$. One obtains:

$$\phi_{\upsilon | pa(\upsilon)} | \upsilon_j, \overline{pa}(\upsilon) \sim \mathcal{D}_j[\alpha_1, ..., \alpha_j + 1, ..., \alpha_J] \qquad (28)$$

   i.e., the estimation of the a posteriori distribution of $\phi_{\upsilon | pa(\upsilon)}$ is straightforward.

2. Suppose that both υ and its parents cannot be observed with certainty. Assuming local and global independence, the a posteriori distribution becomes:

$$p(\phi_{\upsilon | \overline{pa}(\upsilon)} | e) = \sum_\vartheta \mathcal{D}_j p(\upsilon_i | \overline{pa}(\upsilon), e) p(\overline{pa}(\upsilon) | e) + \mathcal{D}_0(1 - p(\overline{pa}(\upsilon) | e)) \qquad (29)$$

where $\mathcal{D}_0$ is the initial distribution of $\mathcal{D}[\vartheta_1, ..., \vartheta_J]$. The previous expression provides a combination of the a posteriori distribution with the a priori one corrected by suitable weights. In order to avoid the numerical procedure becomes cumbersome due to the lack of some data, the result is approximated by a Dirichlet distribution with the same moments of the distribution in equation (29).

4.3 Implementation

The code BAIES solves the indetermination of the moment to be assumed as reference in the last approximation by using the average variance. All the steps described in this section are already operative within BAIES.

The implementation of a learning procedure in the object-oriented code is still in progress on the basis of a feasibility study that can be summarized as follows. The marginal probabilities of each node υ, $p(\upsilon)$, are already computed and stored by the algorithm. Moreover, the computation of the joint distribution of υ and pa(υ), $p(\upsilon, pa(\upsilon))$, has been added. The knowledge of the latter distribution allows one to write:

$$p(\upsilon | pa(\upsilon)) = \frac{p(\upsilon, pa(\upsilon))}{p(\upsilon)} \qquad (30)$$

and this activates the updating formulae of the learning process.

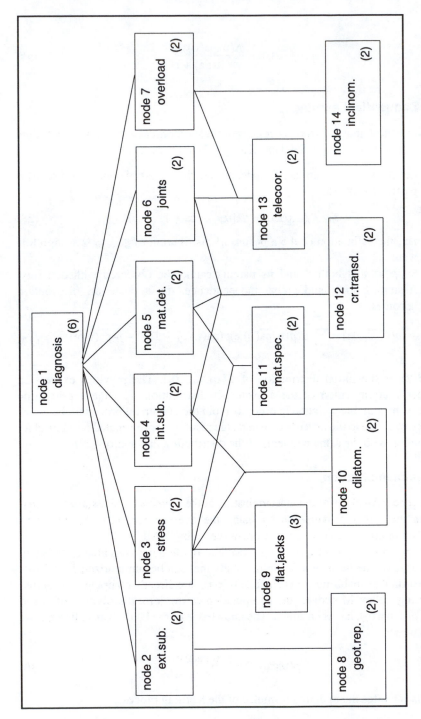

Figure 2. Oriented acyclic graph for the numerical experiment: the number between brackets is the number of states of the discrete variable associated with each node.

5. A NUMERICAL EXAMPLE

Figure 2 shows the oriented acyclic graph for the structural diagnosis example developed in this article. There is a spectrum of six limit states: each of them has links with seven quantities which can be measured, observed and/or monitored. The total number of nodes is 14. The limit-state nodes express, by means of two states, yes, Y, and no, N, the presence of:

1. external subsidence (node 2) influenced by the geotechnical report (node 8);
2. excessive stress (node 3) influenced by the results of tests executed by flat jacks (node 9), dilatometers (node 10) and material specimens (node 11);
3. internal subsidence (node 4) influenced by the readings of the dilatometers (node 10) and the readings of the transducers at the cracks (node 12);
4. material deterioration (node 5) influenced by the results on the material specimens (node 11) and by the readings of the crack transducers (node 12);
5. inadequate joints between vertical and horizontal elements (node 6) influenced by the measures of the crack transducers (node 12) and of the telecoordinometer (node 13);
6. overload (node 7) detected by the telecoordinometer (node 13) and the top inclinometer (node 14).

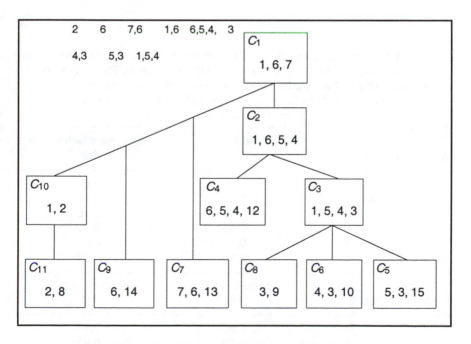

Figure 3. Joint tree for the graph of Figure 2.

Each of the six intermediate nodes corresponds to a load effect to be compared with the corresponding strength: the diagnosis consists in classifying the state of health of the structure. The graph transformation leads one to build the joint tree of Figure 3. The qualitative aspects till now considered must then be replaced by quantitative estimates in view of the assessment of the relevant probabilistic structure. An example of subjective evaluation of the conditional probability table is provided in Table 1.

5.1 Evidence Propagation

Once the joint tree of Figure 3 has been obtained, one considers the adjacent cliques C_{10} and C_{11}, made by the nodes 1, 2 and 2, 8, respectively, with node 2 as separator element. The tables of the initial potentials are given in Table 2. Its first column provides the conditional probabilities p(node 8|node 2) for C11 and p(node 2|node 1) for C_{10}. If one incorporates the evidence { e : geotech. rep. = Y }, the potentials modify as in the second column of Table 2. They, in fact must be multiplied by the updating ratio between the values of the potentials of the separation element (0.9/1. and 0.05/1., respectively). The values of the potentials of the clique C_{10} given in the third column take into account an equi-probable initial condition at node 1: this third column also provides the transfer from the top clique to the bottom one. The fourth column gives the marginal distributions after normalization.

Table 1. Subjective Evaluation of the Conditional Probability Associated with the Links (node 1 → node 2) and (node 2 → node 8). The Diagnosis Concerns with an Anomalous State of Stress, External Subsidence, Internal Subsidence, Material Deterioration, Overload and Joints.

node 1: limit state ?	node 2: Yes	ext. subsidence ? No
stress	0.10	0.90
ex. subsidence	0.90	0.10
in. subsidence	0.05	0.95
material det.	0.05	0.95
overload	0.10	0.90
joints	0.10	0.90

node 2: ext. sub. ?	node 8: Yes	geotech. rep. ? No
Yes	0.90	0.10
No	0.05	0.95

Table 2. Propagation of Evidence Through the Cliques C_{10} and C_{11}: Initial Potential, Evidence Incorporation, Final Potentials, Marginal Tables (Evidence on the Geotechnical Report).

	C_{10}							
limit state	ext.s		ext.s		ext.s		ext.s	
	Y	N	Y	N	Y	N	Y	N
stress	0.10	0.90	.090	.045	.0150	.0075	.064	.032
ex. subsidence	0.90	0.10	.810	.0050	.1350	.000833	.577	.004
in. subsidence	0.05	0.95	.045	.0475	.0075	.007917	.032	.034
material det.	0.05	0.95	.045	.0475	.0075	.007917	.032	.034
overload	0.10	0.90	.090	.045	.015	.0075	.064	.032
joints	0.10	0.90	.090	.045	.015	.0075	.064	.032
S	1.00	1.00	0.90	0.05	.195	.0392	.833	.167
geotech. rep.								
Yes	0.90	0.05	0.90	0.05	.195	.0392	.833	.167
No	0.10	0.95	0	0	0	0	0	0
	C_{11}							

If one has a double evidence $\{e : \text{geotech. report} = Y + \text{inclinometer} = Y\}$, the third column is modified after the propagation in the network [16]. The results of Table 3 are then derived.

5.2 Learning

When the conditional probabilities are estimated on a subjective basis, a range for them can also be specified: this makes explicit the uncertainty which characterizes these values. An example of ranges for these probabilities is given in Table 4, together with the corresponding values of the variables ϑ_i; the values of Table 2 become in this case the a priori means of the parameter ϕ_v.

Table 5 illustrates the updatings of the a priori distribution $\phi_{\text{ext. sub.|diagnosis}} = \text{ext. sub.}$ for different cases of evidence.

6. CONCLUSIONS

A learning strategy is incorporated into a generic expert system devoted to the detection of the state of soundness of existing structures. It makes use of the same governing relations of the theory of causal probabilistic networks [21, 22].

Table 3. Propagation of Evidence Through the Cliques C_{10} and C_{11}:
Initial Potential, Evidence Incorporation, Final Potentials, Marginal Tables
(Evidence on the Geotechnical Report and on the Inclinometer).

	C_{10}							
limit state	ext.s		ext.s		ext.s		ext.s	
	Y	N	Y	N	Y	N	Y	N
stress	0.10	0.90	.090	.045	.0033	.00165	.079	.040
ex. subsidence	0.90	0.10	.810	.0050	.0125	.00007	.300	.002
in. subsidence	0.05	0.95	.045	.0475	.0007	.0007	.017	.017
material det.	0.05	0.95	.045	.0475	.0007	.0007	.017	.017
overload	0.10	0.90	.090	.045	.0122	.0061	.293	.146
joints	0.10	0.90	.090	.045	.0020	.0010	.048	.024
S	1.00	1.00	0.90	0.05	.0314	.0103	.753	.247
rap. geot.								
Yes	0.90	0.05	0.90	0.05	.0314	.0103	.753	.247
No	0.10	0.95	0	0	0	0	0	0

C_{11}

Table 4. Subjective Estimation of the Conditional Probabilities Associated
with the Links (node 1 → 2) and (node 2 → 8). The Corresponding Ranges
are Provided Together with Their Translation into Values of the
Parameters $\vartheta 1$ and $\vartheta 2$ of the Beta Distribution (as Calculated by Code BAIES).

	node 2: Yes		ext. sub. ? No	
node 1: limit state ?	range	ϑ_1	range	ϑ_2
stress	.05-.20	0.779	.70-.99	5.260
ex. subsidence	.70-.99	5.260	.05-.20	0.779
in. subsidence	.02-.08	1.280	.90-.99	24.30
material det.	.02-.08	1.280	.90.99	24.3
overload	.05-.20	0.779	.70-.99	5.260
joints	.05-.20	0.779	.70-.99	5.260

	node 8: Yes		geotech. rep. ? No	
node 2: subsidence ?	range	ϑ_1	range	ϑ_2
Yes	.80-.99	9.320	.02-.15	0.890
No	.01-.10	1.410	.90-.99	24.26

Table 5. Updatings of the a Priori Distribution $\phi_{ext. sub.|diagnosis=ext. sub.}$
for Different Cases of Evidence

A priori	ϑ_1	ϑ_2
distribution $\mathcal{D}_0$	5.26	.779
$\mathcal{D}_1$ e: ext.sub. = Y + diagnosis=ext. sub.	6.26	.779
$\mathcal{D}_2$ e: ext.sub. = N + diagnosis=ext. sub.	5.26	.178
e: geotech. rep. = Y + diagnosis=ext. sub.	6.19	.777
e: geotech. rep. = Y	5.70	.770

The examples were conceived for the structural diagnosis of monumental buildings but the applications can easily be extended to other fields as fire detection or structural diagnosis after a fire event. Causal probabilistic networks can also be useful for the identification of repair priorities.

Research continues toward two further objectives:

1. the implementation of the learning algorithm into the object programming software presently available;
2. the conception and development of graphs of actual support to specific applications of structural diagnosis.

REFERENCES

1. M. Chiogna, *Approcci alternativi al problema di classificazione: una applicazione in ambito medico* (in Italian), Ph.D. Thesis, Dip. di Scienze Statistiche, Università di Padova, Italy, 1993.
2. Y. Reich and S. J. Fenves, The Potential of Machine Learning Techniques for Expert Systems, *Artificial Intelligence in Engineering Design Analysis, 3*:3, pp. 175-193, 1989.
3. F. Casciati and L. Faravelli, *Fragility Analysis of Complex Structural Systems*, Research Studies Press, Taunton, United Kingdom, 1991.
4. L. Faravelli and P. Gherardini, Seismic History at Monumental Sites by AI Working Environment, in *Repair and Maintenance of Historical Buildings*, Seville, (Spain), Vol. II, pp. 65-76, 1991.
5. L. Faravelli and P. Gherardini, *Consulting Data Banks of Seismic Events and Damages,* proceeding Workshop on Application of Artificial Intelligence Techniques in Seismology and Engineering Seismology, Luxembourg, 1992.
6. L. Faravelli and P. Gherardini, Expert System Modules for System Control, in *Intelligent Structures II*, Y. K. Wen (ed.), Elsevier, pp. 128-143, 1992.
7. F. Casciati and L. Faravelli, *Exploiting Expertise in Monumental Building Diagnosis,* proceedings of 10th WCEE, Madrid, *10*, pp. 6283-6289, 1992.
8. D. J. Speigelhalter, A. P. Dawid, S. L. Lauritzen, and R. G. Cowel, *Bayesian Analysis in Expert Systems*, BAIES report BR 27, MRC Biostatistic Unit, Cambridge, 1992.

9. G. Augusti, A. Baratta, and F. Casciati, *Probabilistic Methods in Structural Engineering*, Chapman & Hall, London, 1984.

10. F. Casciati and L. Faravelli, Causal Probabilistic Networks in Assessing the Vulnerability of Existing Buildings, in *Structural Engineering in Natural Hazard Mitigation*, ASCE, pp. 1318-1323, 1993.

11. F. Casciati and L. Faravelli, *Learning Process for Structural-Engineering Artificial-Intelligence Tools,* proceedings of ECC Workshop on Artificial Intelligence and Expert Systems Training in Structures, Athens, January 9-12, 1994.

12. F. Casciati and L. Faravelli, A Knowledge-Based System for Seismic Vulnerability Assessment of Masonry Buildings, *Microcomputers in Civil Engineering, 6,* pp. 291-301, 1992.

13. F. Casciati and L. Faravelli, *Expert Systems and Seismic Vulnerability,* proceedings 9th ECEE, Moscow, *I*, pp. 23-32, 1990.

14. D. A. Reed, Treatment Uncertainty in Structural Damage Assessment, *Reliability Engineering and System Safety, 39*, pp. 55-64, 1993.

15. F. Casciati, L. Faravelli, and P. Gherardini, *Sistemi esperti e trattazione dell'incertezza: uno stato dell'arte* (in Italian), Dip. Meccanica Strutturale, Università di Pavia, UNIPAV-MS-2-91, 1991.

16. F. Casciati and L. Faravelli, *Reti causali probabilistiche con apprendimento: uno strumento decisionale per la diagnosi strutturale* (in Italian), Dip. Meccanica Strutturale, Università di Pavia, UNIPAV-MS-2-93, 1994.

17. R. G. Cowell, *BAIES—A User's Guide*, Department of Statistical Science, University College, London, 1992.

18. Neuron Data, *Nexpert Object Reference Manuals*, Palo Alto, California, 1991.

19. P. Gherardini, *Implementazione object-oriented di un modello di calcolo per reti causali* (in Italian), proceedings of the XXXV Riun. Scient. SIS. Cedam, Padova, 1991.

20. N. L. Johnson and S. Kotz, *Distribution in Statistics: Continuous Multivariate Distributions*, John Wiley, 1972.

21. S. L. Lauritzen and D. J. Spiegelhalter, Local Computations with Probabilities on Graphical Structures and Their Application to Expert Systems (with Discussion), *Journal of Royal Statistical Society, 50*, pp. 157-224, 1988.

22. D. J. Spieghelhalter and S. L. Lauritzen, Sequential Updating of Conditional Probabilities on Directed Graphical Structures, *Networks, 20*, pp. 579-605, 1990.

CHAPTER 6

Limitations of Fire Models

Alan N. Beard

The limitations of computer-based fire models are considered in very general terms. The main different kinds of deterministic models are considered, that is "zone models" and CFD-based models. The vital importance of the appropriate use of a model and suitable interpretation of results is stressed. Inappropriate use of fire models in fire safety decision-making may be dangerous. Some general conclusions are drawn.

During the last twenty-five years there has been a great increase in the construction of computer-based models related to fire risk. In general, the purpose of such models is to enable better assessment of the fire risk in a given case with particular types of occupants, contents, and building design. In principle, they should help in estimating some of the likely effects of making a change to a system, whether new or existing.

During the 1970s the dominant paradigm for such models was the probabilistic one, although much deterministic work did take place. During the 1980s the probabilistic paradigm tended to be replaced by the deterministic one, although probabilistic work did continue. During the 1990s and into the next millennium it is to be hoped that a synthesis of the two approaches will start to come about; the best being reaped from each paradigm. In general, this would be a desirable development and there are tentative signs that this may be starting to come about.

General conclusions are very difficult to arrive at. However, one thing can be said with certainty and that is that this whole field is changing very rapidly.

The general question emerges of what is an appropriate role for such fire models and this article attempts to make a contribution as part of an answer to this question. A central theme which emerges is the need to avoid the danger of seeing a model in isolation, as a *deus ex machina*. It is necessary to guard against the emergence of a "fetishism of models" in our attitude and to try to adumbrate what might be a suitable place for computer-based fire models as part of the decision-making process.

TYPES OF MODELS

Basically, there are two types of theoretical models: deterministic and probabilistic. In a probabilistic model a range of possible developments is allowed for, a probability being associated with each, e.g., the model for fire in a hospital ward of reference [1]. A deterministic model predicts a single possible development. Probabilistic models are desirable to the extent that, in principle, they allow for the sheer complexity of the real world; however, the input data (transition probabilities and temporal distributions) are generally difficult to construct reliably. Deterministic models are desirable to the extent that they may help to shed light on specific processes; however, the predicted course of development may be at great variance with reality. Also, the numerical input to deterministic models may be very uncertain. In both deterministic and probabilistic models the assumptions may be unrealistic.

The remainder of this chapter will focus on deterministic models as these have come into great prominence in recent years. The primary types of deterministic models are zone models and field models.

QUALITATIVE AND QUANTITATIVE ASPECTS
OF MODELS

Two aspects are important when considering a model: qualitative and quantitative. Qualitative aspects refer to conceptual assumptions and ranges of applicability as well as the general trends emerging from results. Quantitative aspects refer to how well a model predicts the magnitudes of quantitative variables in a real case.

Qualitative Aspects

Zone Models

Zone models assume the formation of a very small number of "zones." In particular, this type of model assumes that the smoke forms a homogeneous layer of uniform temperature, smoke density, and gas concentration. Generally, they consider the formation of two zones; an upper layer and a lower layer. The assumption of distinct stratification means that zone models are only applicable to cases in which two clearly defined zones are likely to form. The exact conditions in which this is likely to be so are not well understood. However, it seems to be usually accepted that two zones have a good chance of forming if the room is of rectangular cuboidal shape and is of "domestic size." Even under these conditions it may well be the case that two zones do not form. For example, whether or not two distinct zones are formed may well depend upon the rate of development of the fire. Work needs to be conducted in order to better identify those conditions under which a definite upper layer is likely to be created. That would help to identify those conditions under which zone models are likely to be of value.

Field Models

Field models do not assume a very small number of zones but a variation of the "field variables" (temperature, gas concentrations etc.) throughout the space of concern. In practice a compartment is divided into a large number of cells (typically thousands) and uniformity of conditions is assumed within each cell. In this sense, a field model may be thought of as a zone model but with thousands of zones instead of, essentially, two. In principle, therefore, values of the field variables may be calculated at a very large number of places throughout a building. Also, in principle, there is no limitation on the size or shape of building which may be modeled. A limitation of field models is the very large amount of computing power and time which they require by comparison with zone models.

Sub-Models

Beyond the limitations of the overall conceptual assumptions of a given model there are limitations due to the assumptions in explicit or implicit sub-models, for example, assumptions in relation to heat release rate or production of toxic gases. For example, a zone model assumes a specific sub-model for the flow rate in the plume, whereas a field model assumes a specific model for the turbulence. Which sub-model is used in each case affects the results. As an example, use of the McCaffrey expression for flow rate in the plume above a fire may produce about twice the amount predicted from using the Zukoski expression [2]. For a field model, use of a standard k-ε turbulence model may produce quite different results to those obtained from using a modified k-ε model [3]. By way of illustration, the general qualitative features of three zone models and one field model are summarized in Tables 1, 2, and 3.[1] The three zone models considered are ASET [4], FAST [5], and FIRST [6]. The field model considered is JASMINE Version 1.2 [7]. Each of these models contains sub-models and these should be thoroughly assessed in themselves. In general, it cannot be assumed that sub-models are necessarily reliable. Beyond that, the effects on the results of the model as a whole of making different conceptual assumptions should be investigated, for example, the effect of making different conceptual assumptions in a radiation sub-model.

---

[1] Tables 1, 2, and 3 are reprinted from the *Fire Safety Journal 18*, pp. 375-392, 1992 with kind permission from Elsevier Science Ltd., The Boulevard, Langford Lane, Kidlington OX5 1GB.

Table 1. Key Design Features and Processes

	ASET	HAZARD-I	FIRST	JASMINE (Version 1.2)
Fire Growth (a) 1st Item	■ User injects heat release	■ User injects heat release	●	■ User injects heat release rate
(b) 2nd Item	■ As above	■ As above	●	■ User injects heat release rate
(c) Flashover	■ If associate with given U.L. temp.	■ If associate with given U.L. temp.	■ If associate with given U.L. temp.	■ If associate with given temp. at ceiling
Vents	○	●	●	●
Multi-Compart.	○	●	○	●
Temperature	●	●	●	●
Smoke/Gas Concentrations	●	●	●	●
Radiative Feedback to Fire	○	○	●	○
Egress (via EXITT)	○	●	○	○
Detection (via DETACT)	■ If associate detection with a U.L. conc. or temp.	●	■ If associate with given U.L. temp. of conc.	■ If associate with given temp. or conc.
Fire Resistance	○	■ If associate with given wall temp.	■ If associate with given wall temp.	■ If associate with given wall temp.

Note: ● = Included explicitly, ○ = Not included, ■ = Included implicitly (see comment).

Table 2. Compartment Size and Shape

	ASET	HAZARD-I	FIRST	JASMINE
Compartment Shape	Rectangular Cuboid			Any
Compartment Size	"Domestic-Sized"			Any

Table 3. Key Theoretical Structure

	ASET	HAZARD-I	FIRST	JASMINE
Assumed State	Important Quasi-Steady Elements (Gradual change from Steady State to Steady State)			Unsteady
Degree of Resolution	Zone Model (Small number of zones assumed; mainly 2)			Field (Thousands of zones)

Qualitative Aspects; in Summary

Overall, therefore, the conceptual assumptions in a model will generally affect the results and this needs to be realized and borne in mind when results are considered.

Quantitative Aspects

A given model, with a given conceptual structure, requires a given set of parameters to be assigned numbers as input. This leads to uncertainty associated with:

- Numerical input associated with physical parameters—For example, associated with thermal conductivities or emissivities. There would be much leeway in deciding on "plausible" input values and these may produce quite different results.
- Numerical solution techniques—Different numerical solution techniques lead to different results. For example, a differential equation may be solved using the Runge-Kutta method or the Bulirsch-Stoer method and generally

these produce similar results; however sometimes their results may be quite different. It has also been found that chaos exists in the Newton-Raphson technique [8].

Concerning field models, it has been generally found that the results depend significantly, sometimes dramatically, on the number of cells used [9].

- Software error—In general, mistakes will exist in complicated software. This will usually apply to fire models. It has been estimated that, typically, there could be around eight errors per thousand lines of source code and even for safety-critical code there could be around four errors per thousand lines of code [10]. Any one of these errors could be important, possibly crucial.

- Hardware faults—Whether justifiable or not, in the past, hardware has generally been assumed to be extremely reliable. However, this cannot necessarily be assumed to be the case. The view has been expressed that people will be "killed or injured as a pretty direct effect of mistakes in complex software or mistakes in the design of micro-chips" [11]. This is because of the ever-increasing complexity of microprocessors. Also, there is the well-known case of the failure of the Pentium chip [12], as an example.

- Application error—In addition to the above there is the possibility of an error during insertion of input or reading of output. It has been said that this is a very common occurrence [13].

On top of this is the issue of misinterpretation of results by a user in a particular case; that is a vital but different matter.

COMPARISON WITH EXPERIMENT

A predicted value of a variable such as temperature cannot be compared directly with the actual temperature in a fire. The best that can be done is to compare with experimental results. That may sound simple, but in fact it is not. Experimental results are not absolute but are relative to a number of factors associated with the experiment [9, 14]. These are:

1. Uncertainty associated with lack of controlled conditions.
2. Uncertainty and flexibility associated with the experimental design. For example, where the thermocouples are put.
3. Uncertainty associated with direct error in measurement.
4. Uncertainty associated with raw data processing algorithms. How the raw data are processed to produce a variable of concern, e.g., an average temperature, affects the results.

As an example of the kind of case which arises, see the results in Figure 1. These are from ostensibly identical tests and yet it is clear that the results are very different. The results are from a very well-respected laboratory; it is the kind of

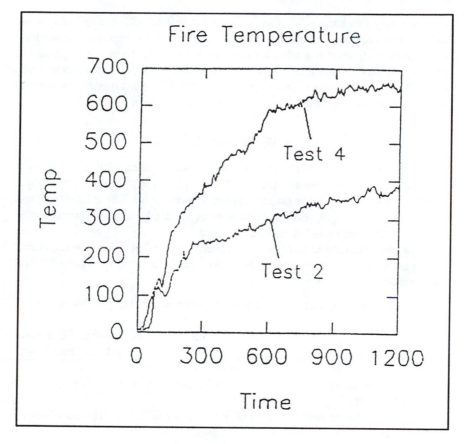

Figure 1. "Identical tests."

thing which does happen and we need to be aware of it. Experimental results are not carved in stone.

COMPARISONS AMONG MODELS

A proposition which emerges from the considerations so far is that a good correspondence between the results from a computer model and a single set of experimental results does not necessarily mean that the model is a good one. Vice versa, a bad correspondence between a single run of a computer model and a single set of experimental results does not necessarily mean that the model is a bad one.

Alternative propositions may be considered: might we assume, for a given model, that the predictions will be consistently higher or lower than experiment?

Unfortunately this cannot be taken to be the case [9]. Alternatively, might we assume that predictions from one model are consistently higher or lower than predictions from another model, for equivalent cases? Unfortunately not, as the results in Table 4 illustrate [15]. This shows simulations applied to the same cases using the same input data as far as possible. Of the three zone models considered, no consistency of one model relative to another can be seen.

USE OF A MODEL

It is apparent that if a model is to be used responsibly, then whatever else might be necessary, sensitivity studies are essential. In a given application then the input should be varied over wide ranges and the effects found. These results should then be seen in the light of the assumptions of the model and interpreted within the context of other knowledge and experience.

Fallacious reasoning such as that associated with the "fifth window argument" would need to be avoided as far as possible. The "fifth window argument" may be summarized as:

1. A room has five open windows and there is a noisy pneumatic drill in use outside.
2. The first window is closed and it is found to make no significant difference to the noise level inside. Likewise for the second, third, and fourth windows; each closed one after the other.
3. The fifth window is closed, which causes a dramatic reduction in the noise inside.
4. It is concluded that it is alright to open the first four windows because closing each of those made no difference.

The "fifth window argument" is an illustration of how easy it is, with reductionistic reasoning, to draw erroneous conclusions; the results of varying a factor must be seen in relation to the values and conditions associated with all other factors.

Table 4. Zone Model Temperature Predictions[a]

Ranking of Predicted Temperature	Test		
	Foam Slab	House	Department Store
Highest	FIRST	FAST	ASET
Middle		ASET	FAST
Lowest	FAST	FIRST	FIRST

[a]Ranking of predicted upper layer temperatures. ASET has not been included for the Foam Slab Test as that model is only intended to apply to closed compartments.

SOME GENERAL CONCLUSIONS

It has become apparent that the issue at present is not so much whether a model is good or bad in absolute terms but rather whether or not a model has the *potential* to assist in the process of gaining a better understanding in a given case. If a model does have a potential in this way, then whether or not the results are valuable or misleading depends upon the case to which it is applied and how the results are used and interpreted. In practical terms we need:

A Model Examination Group

A procedure needs to be devised for assessing fire models which are intended to be used as part of fire safety decision making. Such an assessment procedure would need to be generally agreed and acceptable to society as a whole. As part of this, Model Examination Groups might be established and an agreed methodology for assessment applied. The methodology would cover qualitative and quantitative aspects. Assessment of a given model would need to be conducted by people who are independent of interests associated with a model. That is, by people who have not been involved in the development of the model under consideration and who do not have a particular interest in seeing the model portrayed as "good" or "bad." Such assessment would need to be continual.

In this vein the Home Office commissioned a study of four fire models, i.e., ASET, HAZARD-I, FIRST, and JASMINE version 1.2 between 1988 and 1990 [15]. The guidance resulting from this study has been published as documents [16, 17]. Also, a working group under the title the *Fire Models Context Group* has been meeting under the aegis of the Home Office with the intention of pursuing in practical terms the problems raised by the use of fire models in real-world decision making.

Methodology of Use

If it has been decided that a given model has a potential to be valuable and that it may be used as part of fire safety decision making, then it is imperative that the model be employed in an acceptable way. Acceptable "methodologies of use" need to be devised which would be such as to try to avoid the danger of misinterpretation. For example, sensitivity studies would need to be a fundamental part of the methodology.

An example of a methodology of use which has been devised for the use of models in relation to structural analysis is the SAFESA method [18].

Knowledgeable Use

Even having a model which is accepted as being of potential value and with an acceptable methodology of use; the methodology may still be misused. It is necessary for the methodology of use to be employed in a competent and coherent way and for all results to be seen within the light of the limitations of the model and in the context of other fire knowledge and experience. This is vital.

CONCLUSION

Given suitable action in relation to the three areas above, it is to be hoped that fire models may come to play a valuable role within fire safety decision making. Without suitable action, the use of fire models may turn out to be dangerous.

REFERENCES

1. A. N. Beard, A Stochastic Model for the Number of Deaths in a Fire, *Fire Safety Journal, 4,* pp. 169-184, 1981.
2. C. L. Beyler, Fire Plumes & Ceiling Jets, *Fire Safety Journal, 11,* pp. 53-75, 1986.
3. P. J. Woodburn, *Comparison of Numerical & Experimental Results for a Fire in a Tunnel, 1994,* work conducted for the Health & Safety Executive, current address of author (1996), Department of Civil Engineering, Edinburgh University.
4. L. Y. Cooper, A Mathematical Model for Estimating Available Safe Egress Time, *Fire & Materials, 6,* pp. 135-144, 1982.
5. W. W. Jones, A Multi-Compartment Model for the Spread of Fire, Smoke and Toxic Gases, *Fire Safety Journal, 9,* pp. 55-79, 1985.
6. H. E. Mitler and J. E. Rockett, *User's Guide to FIRST,* NBSIR 87-3595, BFRL, NIST, Washington, D.C., 1987.
7. JASMINE version 1.2, produced by Fire Research Station, Garston, Watford, Hertfordshire, studied by A. N. Beard in *Evaluation of Fire Models,* Reports 5 and 10, conducted for the Home Office, 1990.
8. W. H. Press et al., *Numerical Recipes,* Cambridge University Press, 1992.
9. A. N. Beard, Limitations of Computer Modelling, contained in *Fire Safety Modelling & Building Design,* conference held at University of Salford, March 29, 1994, Department of Surveying, University of Salford, Salford, United Kingdom.
10. D. Jackson, Quoted during presentation on *New Developments in Quality Management as a Pre-Requisite to Safety,* Safety-Critical Systems Symposium, Bristol, February 9-11, 1993, organized by Safety-Critical Systems Club, c/o Centre for Software Reliability, University of Newcastle.
11. J. Cullyer, Warwick University, quoted in *When the Chips are Down,* L. Clifford (ed.), *Systems International, 18,* pp. 42-44, 1990.
12. C. Arthur, Flawed Chips Bug Angry Users, *New Scientist,* p. 18, December 10, 1994.
13. Quoted during discussion at conference: *Safer Computing-Managing Technical Risks,* Institution of Structural Engineers, London, January 30, 1996.
14. A. N. Beard, Limitations of Computer Models, *Fire Safety Journal, 18,* pp. 375-391, 1992.
15. A. N. Beard, *Evaluation of Fire Models—Report 11: Overview,* on research conducted for the Home Office, 1990.

16. B. T. Hume, *Evaluation of Fire Models—Summary Report,* Research Report Number 52, Fire R & D Group, Home Office, London, 1992.

17. B. T. Hume, *Fire Models—A Guide for Fire Prevention Officers,* Fire R & D Group, Publication Number 6/93, Home Office, 1993.

18. N. C. Knowles and J. R. Maguire, On the Qualification of Safety Critical Structures—The SAFESA Approach, *3rd Safety Critical Systems Symposium,* Brighton, February 7-9, 1995, organized by Centre for Software Reliability, University of Newcastle.

CHAPTER 7

The Numerical Simulation of Fire Spread Within a Compartment Using an Integrated Gas and Solid Phase Combustion Model

F. Jia, E. R. Galea, and M. K. Patel

An integrated fire spread model is presented in this study including several sub-models representing different phenomena of gaseous and solid combustion. The integrated model comprises of the following sub-models: a gaseous combustion model, a thermal radiation model that includes the effects of soot, and a pyrolysis model for charring combustible solids. The interaction of the gaseous and solid phases are linked together through the boundary conditions of the governing equations for the flow domain and the solid region respectively. The integrated model is used to simulate a fire spread experiment conducted in a half-scale test compartment. Good qualitative and reasonable quantitative agreement is achieved between the experiment and numerical predictions.

Solid fuel combustion is of central importance to fire research. By its very nature, this involves physical and chemical processes in both the solid and gaseous phases. For a specified room fire scenario, it is desirable to predict the fire development in terms of measurable material properties, the geometric configuration of the compartment and the physical state of the environment. Over the past ten years considerable effort has been expended in developing fire field models [1] capable of predicting the development of hazardous conditions within fire enclosures [1-7].

The majority of practical fire modeling applications have been concerned with the spread of heat and smoke in complex structures and so the combustion process has either been ignored or greatly simplified. In cases where combustion is ignored the fire is treated as a simple time dependent prescribed source of heat and smoke. Generally, when combustion is included, it is approximated using relatively simple one-step reaction mechanisms [8] for gaseous or liquid fuels such as methane.

While some recent work has attempted to predict fire spread in enclosures through the use of zone and field models [9-11], these have incorporated the rate of flame spread over the solid fuel through the use of thermal analysis, empirical formulations, or direct use of Cone Calorimeter data. A different approach [12-15] has been developed where the flame spread is governed by a set of partial differential equations that describe and link gas-phase and solid-phase behavior. In particular, by incorporating a simple pyrolysis model within a fire field model, the authors [12, 13] have attempted to demonstrate the model by simulating the flame spread over a plywood ceiling in a hypothetical room fire scenario. The model was also able to demonstrate the onset of behavior similar to flashover and backdraft. In another demonstration of the models capability, model predictions were compared with experimental data for the combustion of polymethylmeth-acrylate (PMMA) slabs [14]. This model involved a radiation model, a gaseous combustion model, and a (non-charring) pyrolysis model [12-14], all within the framework provided by a field model [1]. However, the treatment lacked the incorporation of a char model.

Flame spread over a combustible solid fuel is dependent on the rate at which combustible gaseous fuels are generated, i.e., the pyrolysis rate, and the rate at which the layer of char residue is formed. Recently, the authors [16] have developed a numerical technique to solve a simple charring pyrolysis model based on the ignition temperature concept that is widely used by other researchers [15, 17, 18]. In a demonstration of the charring pyrolysis model, the authors used the model to simulate the mass loss process from a white pine sample exposed to a constant radiative flux in a nitrogen atmosphere. Comparison with experimental results demonstrated that the predictions of mass loss rates and temperature profile within the solid material were in reasonable agreement with experimental observations [16]. This comparison was performed with the charring pyrolysis model in stand-alone format, i.e., the model was not incorporated within a CFD based fire field model. In this article the authors combine the charring pyrolysis model [16] with a fire field model and compare predictions for a compartment fire with experimental data. Through the introduction of a simple char model, it is hoped that fire field models incorporating solid fuel combustion can produce more realistic predictions.

The primary aim of this work is to develop a practical engineering fire field model that is capable of addressing some of the issues concerning solid fuel combustion. Thus, relatively simple sub-models for radiation and combustion models are considered here.

In the remainder of this chapter the integrated fire model is presented along with a comparison of model predictions with experimental results. In section 2, the sub-models used in the integrated fire spread model, namely the gas-phase combustion model, the thermal radiation model and the charring pyrolysis model, are briefly outlined. In section 3, a fire test used to validate the integrated fire model is described. Experimental results and numerical predictions for the fire test are presented in section 4 along with a discussion of the results. Finally, some concluding remarks are presented.

2. MODEL DESCRIPTION

The flame spread model presented here for a compartment fire is an integrated model within the framework of the CFD software CFDS-FLOW3D version 2.3.3 [2, 19] (later versions of this software are known as CFX). The entire model consists of the following sub-components, a gas-phase combustion model (utilizing the eddy dissipation concept), a radiation model (the six-flux model and the discrete transfer method), and a thermal pyrolysis model (non-charring or charring models). Each individual model has been described in detail and verified in other publications [12-14, 16, 20]. Here only a brief description of these sub-models is presented.

2.1 The Gas-Phase Model

The governing equations for all fluid variables can be expressed in the general form:

$$\frac{\partial \rho \phi}{\partial t} + \text{div}(\rho \vec{U} \phi) = \text{div}(\Gamma_\phi \nabla \phi) + S_\phi \qquad (1)$$

where S_ϕ is the source term and ϕ stands for any one of the following variables: the velocities u, v, w in three coordinate directions, the enthalpy h, the turbulent kinetic energy k, its dissipation rate ε, the mixture fraction ξ, the mass fraction of fuel m_f, and the soot mass fraction m_{soot}. For the continuity equation ϕ takes the value of one. The CFD framework is provided by the general purpose CFD software product CFDS-FLOW3D V2.3.3 [2, 19].

Combustion in the gaseous phase is modeled using the eddy dissipation concept (EDC) [21]. A simple one-step chemical reaction, i.e., $F + v_o O \rightarrow (1+v_o)P$ is assumed. The Lewis number is assumed to be one. The source term of the governing equation for mass fraction of fuel employs the eddy dissipation concept, i.e.,

$$R_f = A \, min(\overline{C}_f, \overline{C}_o /s) \, \frac{\varepsilon}{k} \qquad (2)$$

where A takes the value 4.0, s is the stoichiometric ratio of oxidant to fuel and $\overline{C}_f$ and $\overline{C}_o$ are the concentrations of fuel and oxidant respectively. It should be emphasized that the EDC does not include detailed chemical kinetics, as such the model is not sensitive to temperature and oxygen concentration. The simulated combustion reaction occurs within a computational cell if oxygen and fuel coexist. Consequently, the model ignores the detailed mechanisms of ignition and extinction.

An empirical-based soot model has been incorporated within the combustion model [20]. The soot model used in this study is based on the fact that soot formation takes place in the fuel rich side of chemical reaction region and the highest soot concentration is found in the same region [22-24]. The measured mean soot concentration in the region of soot formation is considered as a final result of the soot formation processes: nucleation, surface growth, coagulation, and oxidation. Therefore, in this region soot concentrations are assumed to remain constant, taking the measured mean values. Outside the soot formation region it is assumed that soot formation and oxidation has ceased due to the lower temperatures and soot particles are transported by convection. An arbitrarily small value is assigned to the diffusion coefficient of this scalar since the soot particles do not diffuse due to the difference of the soot concentration. The soot volume fraction (f_v), used primarily for the radiation calculation, is obtained by

$$f_v = m_{soot} \rho / \rho_{soot}, \tag{3}$$

where ρ and ρ_{soot} are the densities of the gas mixture and the soot respectively. A constant soot density (2000 kg/m^3) [25] is used.

2.2 The Thermal Radiation Model

Thermal radiation is the dominant mode of heat transfer in compartment fires. Thermal radiation from the fire and hot upper gas layer can heat the surrounding combustible materials to their pyrolysis temperature and provide the energy required for the pyrolysis process. In the integrated fire spread model, two options for the radiation model are provided—the six-flux model [26] and the discrete transfer method [27].

As a first approximation, the six-flux model is used to describe thermal radiation. This model has successfully been applied to a number of practical problems involving radiation [26]. The six radiation fluxes in the positive and negative directions, x, y, z are denoted by F_x^+, F_x^-, F_y^+, F_y^-, F_z^+, and F_z^-, respectively. Let $R_x = F_x^+ + F_x^-$, $R_y = F_y^+ + F_y^-$, $R_z = F_z^+ + F_z^-$. Then R_α is governed by the following second-order ordinary differential equation

$$d[1/a \, dR_\alpha/ds]/ds = S_\alpha, \qquad \alpha = x, y, z \tag{4}$$

where $S_\alpha = R_\alpha(a+s) - 2a\sigma T^4 - s(R_x + R_y + R_z)/3$, a and s are the absorption and scattering coefficients respectively and σ is Stefan-Boltzmann constant.

The primary attraction of this model is that it is easily incorporated into the finite volume scheme of the numerical solution procedure adopted by fire field models and is much less demanding on computational power than other advanced radiation models such as the discrete transfer method.

In the discrete transfer method [27] the radiative transfer equation is solved along a number of prescribed rays. By ignoring the scattering effect, radiation along a ray is determined by

$$\frac{d}{ds} I(\Omega,r) = a\, I(\Omega,r) + aI_b(r) \tag{5}$$

where Ω is the ray direction; s represents the physical pathlength along Ω; r is the position of a point; $I(\Omega, r)$ stands for radiation intensity along Ω at position r; a is the absorption coefficient of the medium.

Each cell through which the ray passes is treated as isothermal. Thus radiation intensity along the ray is represented by the following recurrence relation.

$$I_{n+1} = I_n \exp(-a\delta_s) + [1 - \exp(-a\delta_s)]/I_b \tag{6}$$

where I_n and I_{n+1} are respectively the radiation intensities of entering and leaving the cell through which the ray passes and δ_s is the ray segment within the cell.

Assuming a grey wall surface, the wall boundary is calculated by

$$I = \varepsilon_w I_b/\pi + (1-\varepsilon_w)\Gamma \tag{7}$$

where Γ is the incident radiation intensity at the wall surface.

If sufficient well directed rays are used in the simulation, the discrete transfer method is capable of producing a more accurate representation of radiation than the six-flux model, all-be-it at a higher computational cost.

2.3 The Thermal Pyrolysis Model

Many efforts have been made to understand the chemical and physical processes of pyrolysis. A number of models have been proposed to treat the complex chemical and physical changes in the pyrolyzing solid fuels. Excellent reviews describing the mechanisms and models of the thermal degradation processes were given by Blasi [28] and Kashiwagi [29]. However, there are essentially two approaches to representing pyrolysis, the so-called kinetic and ablative models. The kinetic models try to incorporate the kinetic mechanisms of the thermal degradation of solid fuels. This can lead to a proliferation of complex equations with a heavy reliance on empirical data that is either not available for the particular fuel or unreliable. While ignoring the complex chemical reactions in the pyrolyzing material the ablation models are much simpler than the kinetic models.

This approach can be considered a limit situation of the kinetic regime, i.e., the kinetics of the degradation mechanism by which the solid is converted into gaseous products are assumed at an infinitely fast rate [30]. This approach also has the advantage of requiring only a few quantities describing the condensed phase: the pyrolysis temperature, the heat of pyrolysis, and the thermal inertial properties. Comparisons with experimental results show this approach is capable to producing reasonably good predictions of mass loss rates [12-16, 31, 32]. The aim of this chapter is to develop an integrated flame spread model for engineering applications. The model is therefore expected to be economical and flexibility and capable of a wide range of applications. Thus, the ablation regime of pyrolysis models is selected to simulate the mass loss processes of solid fuels.

Two fundamental assumptions in the ablation models are that solid fuels are gasified only at the surface region (for noncharring materials) or at the char/virgin interface (for charring fuels). Secondly, combustible gaseous products are released only when the solid surface is heated to the critical pyrolysis temperature (ignition temperature) and the temperature of the pyrolyzing regions remains at the pyrolysis temperature throughout the mass loss stage.

In addition, the chemical changes within the pyrolyzing regions are not taken into account. The solid fuel is considered to be chemically inert. The mass transfer in the barrier layer (char or melted film) over virgin material is ignored. Only heat transfer within the condensed phase is treated. The deformation of the fuel due to the thermal expansion and mass loss is neglected. The thermal properties are assumed not to vary with temperature. Under these conditions, the thermal pyrolysis model for charring materials in which the gas/char surface re-radiation losses are considered can be described as follows:

In the char layer

$$\frac{\partial T}{\partial t} = \frac{\partial}{\partial x}\left(\alpha_c \frac{\partial T}{\partial x}\right) \qquad\qquad s < x < l \qquad (8)$$

and in the virgin material

$$\frac{\partial T}{\partial t} = \frac{\partial}{\partial x}\left(\alpha_v \frac{\partial T}{\partial x}\right) \qquad\qquad 0 < x < s \qquad (9)$$

with boundary conditions
a) at the gas/char surface

$$\lambda_c \frac{\partial T_c}{\partial x} = \ddot{q}'' - \ddot{q}''_{rr} \qquad\qquad x = l \qquad (10)$$

where $\ddot{q}''$ includes two parts—the radiative external heat flux, $\ddot{q}''_r$ and the convective heat fluxes $\ddot{q}''_c$ ($h_c(T_a - T_c)$) and $\ddot{q}''_{rr}$ ($\varepsilon\sigma(T_c^4 - T_a^4)$) is the gas/char surface re-radiation losses.
b) at the char/virgin interface

$$T = T_p \qquad\qquad x = s \qquad (11)$$

$$-\lambda_c \frac{\partial T_c}{\partial x} = -\lambda_v \frac{\partial T_v}{\partial x} + \rho L \frac{\partial s}{\partial t} \qquad\qquad x = s \qquad (12)$$

c) at the bottom of the virgin material

$$-\lambda_v \frac{\partial T_v}{\partial x} = 0 \qquad\qquad x = 0 \qquad (13)$$

If heat losses due to surface re-radiation and convection are considered, the boundary condition at the bottom may be altered to

$$-\lambda_v \frac{\partial T_v}{\partial x} = h_c(T_a - T_v) + \varepsilon\sigma(T_a^4 - T_v^4) \qquad x = 0 \qquad (13a)$$

and initial conditions

$$s(0) = l \qquad\qquad (14)$$

$$T(x, 0) = T(x) \qquad\qquad (15)$$

where the initial pyrolysis position is assumed at the top of the solid sample.

Finally, the mass loss rate is obtained by

$$\dot{m}'' = -(\rho_v - \rho_c)\frac{\partial s}{\partial t} \qquad\qquad (16)$$

A decoupling technique to solve this pyrolysis model has been developed to tackle the entanglement of the nonlinear boundary condition and the movement of the char/virgin front for a thermal pyrolysis model for charring materials [16].

2.4 Coupling of the Various Sub-Models

One of the major challenges in this work concerns how to efficiently incorporate the solid field calculations into the framework of CFDS-FLOW3D. Once the surface of the solid fuel is heated to the pyrolysis temperature T_p, it begins to be gasified. The gasified combustible products are allowed to enter the flow domain at the position of the burning solid cell. The rate at which the combustible pyrolysis products enter the flow domain at the position of the burning solid cell is equal to the mass loss rate of the solid fuel at the burning cell determined from the pyrolysis model. It is assumed that the combustible gas is blown-off the solid surface with a zero initial velocity. Once the solid has been gasified, the gaseous combustion model is activated to simulate the flame spread process. For simplicity the gaseous specific heat and molecular weight are assumed to be constants.

Solid mass losses of the target fuel due to gasification are described by regression of the solid surface. It is assumed that the reduction in solid surface does not impact on the gas motion near the solid surface.

The discretization of the solid field is separate from that of the flow domain. The mesh in the solid field can be made completely independent of that in the flow domain. An arbitrary representation of the relationship between flow and solid cells is depicted in Figure 1. Physical quantities—such as heat flux—transferred from the flow domain to a particular solid surface cell must be obtained by averaging the contributions from the flow cells adjacent to the solid cell. Conversely, the contributions from the solid surface to the flow field—such as radiation from the solid or combustible mass flux from the solid cells to the flow—must also be averaged, interpolated, or summed. If computational cells in the solid and gaseous regions do not have a one-to-one correspondence—as shown in Figure 2—then a complex averaging procedure is required in order to preserve conservation. For simplicity and efficiency however, the surface of the solid is discretized according to the discretization of the flow domain, thus maintaining a one-to-one correspondence and resulting is a simplified transfer procedure. While this process fixes the discretization on the surface of the solid fuel, the number of cells along the thickness of the fuel is a free parameter. The number of the cells along the thickness of the solid is determined from a previous one-dimensional mesh sensitivity analysis [20]. The manner in which the solid fuel is discretized is depicted in Figure 2. Although the surface mesh of the solid region is dictated by the discretization of the flow field, the actual computational mesh of cells used to discretize the solid fuel is separated from the flow domain. The mesh for the solid fuel is stored separately to the mesh for the flow domain. The advantage of this treatment is that the relatively fine mesh along the thickness of the solid fuel does not necessarily create a corresponding fine mesh in the flow domain.

Flame spread over the solid surface represents an interaction between gas phase and solid phase combustion. The interplay between the gas phase and solid phase behaviors needs to be carefully dealt with. This interaction is embodied in the boundary conditions on the interface between gas and solid. The boundary conditions for energy are

a) in virgin fuel region (in preheating stage)

$$T = T_s \tag{17}$$

$$\lambda_s \frac{\partial T_s}{\partial n} = \dot{q}_r'' + \dot{q}_c'' - \dot{q}_{rr}'' \tag{18}$$

where $\dot{q}_r''$ and $\dot{q}_c''$ are the radiation heat flux and the convective heat flux at the surface respectively and $\dot{q}_{rr}''$ ($\varepsilon\sigma T_s^4$) is the surface re-radiation losses.

b) in pyrolysis region at the gas/char surface

$$T = T_c \tag{19}$$

$$\lambda_c \frac{\partial T_c}{\partial n} = \dot{q}_r'' + \dot{q}_c'' - \dot{q}_{rr}'' \tag{20}$$

where $\dot{q}_{rr}''$ ($\varepsilon\sigma T_c^4$) is the gas/char surface re-radiation losses.

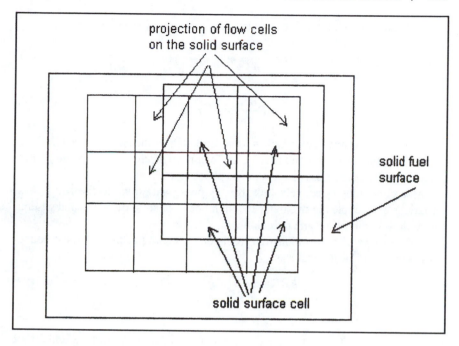

Figure 1. Arbitrary surface relationship between computational cells in the solid and flow regions showing a non one-to-one relationship.

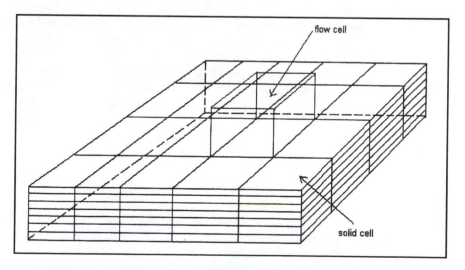

Figure 2. Surface relationship between computational cells in the solid and flow regions showing a one-to-one relationship as used in the present model.

The boundary conditions for mass transfer in the pyrolysis region are

$$\rho D \frac{\partial m_f}{\partial n} = \dot{m}'' (m_f - 1) \tag{21}$$

$$\rho D \frac{\partial m_o}{\partial n} = \dot{m}'' m_o \tag{22}$$

where n is the outward going unit normal direction to the solid surface, λ, D, ρ, m_f, m_o are the thermal conductivity, diffusion coefficient, density, fuel mass fraction, and oxidant mass fraction in gas phase respectively.

These conditions effectively link the gas phase variations to the solid phase variations and couple the two independent models for solid pyrolysis and gaseous phase flow, combustion, and radiation.

At the surface of non-combustible walls or the ceiling or the floor, the boundary condition for heat transfer is

$$k_s \partial T_s / \partial x = \dot{q}_r'' + \dot{q}_c'' - \varepsilon_s \sigma T_s^4 \tag{23}$$

$$T_s = T \tag{24}$$

where k_s, ε_s, and T_s stand respectively for the conductivity, surface emissivity, and temperature of the non-combustible solid, T is the temperature of the gas mixture and $\dot{q}_r''$ and $\dot{q}_c''$ are the radiation flux and convective heat flux at the solid surface respectively. Since the heat losses through the non-combustible walls, floor, or ceiling of a compartment affect the course of the fire spread within the compartment, the temperatures at these non-combustible solid surfaces need evaluation. However, from the computational cost point of view, it is uneconomic and unnecessary to calculate temperature distributions within the non-burning solid walls or ceiling by solving the conduction equation for the solid. A more economical method is required to calculate the solid surface temperature. A relatively simple approach is to use the integral method [33] applied to transient heat conduction in non-combustible solid materials. This technique has been successfully used in previous fire modeling applications [34].

The convective heat flux can be expressed as

$$\dot{q}_c'' = h_c(T_s - T_g) \tag{25}$$

where T_g is the gas main stream temperature near the solid surface and h_c is the convective heat transfer coefficient. The solid surface temperature T_s can be obtained from the pyrolysis model if the solid is combustible or from the integral model [33] if the solid is non-combustible. If the non-combustible solid material is quite thin, for example a glass vision panel, the finite difference method can be employed to obtain the solid surface temperature. The convective heat flux calculated in terms of equation (25) is then used to set up the boundary condition of heat transfer at the solid surface for the flow domain. In fact this reciprocal procedure is placed into the iterative process of the CFDS-FLOW3D software in each time step.

3. SIMULATION OF FIRE SPREAD WITHIN AN ENCLOSURE—CHARRING MATERIAL INVOLVED

Several small scale compartment fire tests were carried out by the Fire Research and Development Group, U.K. Home Office Fire Experimental Unit with the assistance of FSEG [20]. The objectives of the tests were to obtain experimental data of fire spread over ceiling lining material within a small scale compartment. This data was used to verify the integrated fire spread model presented in this article.

3.1 Description of the Experiments

The fire spread tests were conducted in a specially designed half-scale compartment. The internal dimension of the compartment is 1.2 m (wide) × 1.2 m high (long). A schematic of the compartment is shown in Figure 3. The compartment had a door located in the end wall opposite the fire measuring 0.38 m (wide) × 0.99 m (high), the door was open throughout the experiment. The glass vision panel is 1700 mm long by 961 mm high. The inside walls were covered with silver fire blankets. A methane burner is placed inside a steel tray 300 mm ×

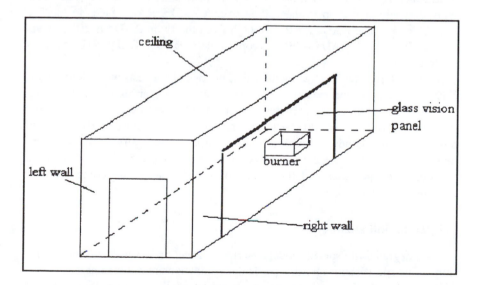

Figure 3. The schematic view of the half scale compartment.

300 mm × 150 mm which is mounted on legs 150 mm high. It was centrally placed 17.5 cm away from the rear wall. A sheet of 18 mm thick standard chipboard measuring 98 cm wide by 235 cm long was suspended beneath the ceiling of the compartment. Strengthening battens were fixed to the back of the sheet to prevent wrapping or sagging of the wood.

A thermocouple tree with five thermocouples labeled from TCT1 to TCT5, was placed at the corner 40 cm from the front wall and 20 cm from the left wall. The heights of the five thermocouple are 20 cm, 40 cm, 60 cm, 80 cm, and 100 cm. To measure the temperature in the hot layer, two thermocouples labeled as TCH1 and TCH2 respectively were installed along the centerline of the chipboard. They were 10 cm below the ceiling and 80 cm and 140 cm away from the front wall respectively. Another four thermocouples were installed close to the left wall. Two of them labeled as TCLW1 and TCLW2 were 30 cm away from the left wall, 90 cm away from the rear wall, and 60 cm and 100 cm above the floor respectively. The other two thermocouples labeled as TCLW3 and TCLW4 were 20 cm from the left wall, 120 cm away from the rear wall, and 60 cm and 100 cm above the floor respectively. Six thermocouples labeled here from TCW1 to TCW6 were used to measure the temperature within the chipboard. They were equally spaced along the centerline of the chipboard at 0.39 m, 0.78 m, 1.17 m, 1.56 m, 1.95 m, and 2.33 m from the rear wall. Each of the thermocouples was fixed at a depth of 2 mm from the front.

Six radiometers were used to measure the radiation heat fluxes at different positions and orientations. They are labeled as RAD1, RAD2, RAD3, RAD4, RAD5, and RAD6. The locations of the radiometers are plotted in Figure 4. All the radiometers faced up to the ceiling except RAD5. RAD5 faces to the fire. RAD1, RAD2, and RAD3 are 21 cm high from the floor. RAD4 is 20 cm away from the right wall, RAD5 is 30 cm from the left wall and RAD6 is 20 cm from the left wall.

A total of five tests were conducted. The first three tests were tentative to find the suitable burner power for this small-scale compartment. Finally it was decided to use a burner output of approximate 48 kW. Test 4 was the first test with the 48 kW burner. In order to check the reproducibility of the experiment an extra test (test 5) was conducted with the same burner power. Very good agreement between the measurements was obtained for the tests 4 and 5. Test 5 was chosen for simulation purposes and the results of the simulation are compared with experimental data.

3.2 Model Initialization

The integrated fire spread model described in section 2 is used for the simulation. Some specifications for this particular simulation are outlined here.

The walls of the compartment are assumed adiabatic since they are well insulated by fire blankets. The glass vision panel and the floor are modeled as

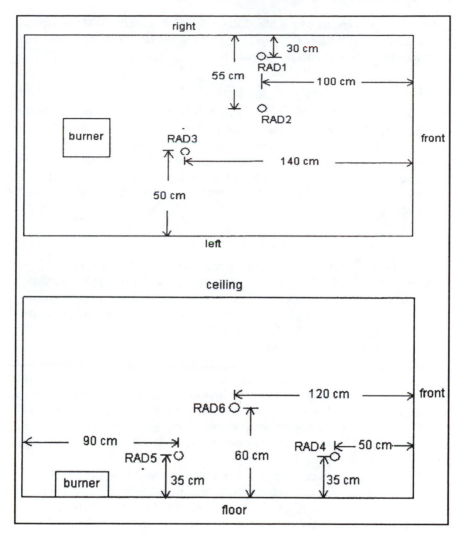

Figure 4. The locations of the radiometers.

conductive regions. The glass temperature is calculated by solving the discretized conduction equation for the glass while the floor temperature is calculated by using the integral method described in section 2.

The burner is simulated as a volumetric heat source of approximately 48 kW. The burner is represented by a rectangular heat source of surface area equal to that of the burner used in the experiment.

For the results presented here, the discrete transfer method (DTM) is used to calculate the radiative heat exchanges. The DTM made use of fifty-four rays. The absorption coefficient of soot is evaluated by

$$\kappa = af_v T \tag{28}$$

where a takes the value of 1275.95 which was determined from previously published experimental data of soot concentration and the absorption coefficient from wood fires [35, 36], f_v and T are the soot volume fraction and temperature of the soot-gas mixture predicted by the model at a point of space. A scalar variable for the soot concentration is used and the soot concentration is calculated from the soot model described in section 2. The absorption coefficient of water and CO_2 used is given by [21]

$$\alpha_g = 0.1(m_c + m_w) \tag{29}$$

where m_c and m_w are the mass concentration of CO_2 and H_2O respectively.

The mass loss of the chipboard is simulated using the charring pyrolysis model described in the previous section. The material properties of chipboard are selected from the literature [15, 37]. The properties used in the simulation are: $\rho_v = 670$ kg/m^3, $C_v = 3000$ J/kgK, $\lambda_v = 0.22$ W/mK, $\lambda_c = 0.17$ W/mK, $T_p = 590$ K, and the pyrolysis heat of 1.3 MJ/kg.

Although smouldering combustion may occur at the initial ignition stage, it is very difficult to simulate this process in the current model. A simple treatment to account for this is to slightly reduce the pyrolysis temperature, to allow combustible gases released slowly when the solid is being exposed to low external heat fluxes. Thus, the pyrolysis temperature of the solid material in the area directly above the burner is reduced from 590 K to 550 K and it is kept at this value throughout the simulation.

The flow domain mesh used in the simulation comprised of 13,320 cells (20 (w) × 18 (h) × 37 (l)). It is non-uniformly distributed with refinement near the walls and the ceiling (see Figure 5). The set-up of the mesh in the combustible solid region has been described in section 2.4, this consisted of a mesh of 26,880 cells (16 (w) × 28 (l) × 60 (d)) with a cell thickness of 0.02 cm.

There are several uncertainties in the simulation. First, the walls and the floor of the compartment are made from composite materials. The heat losses through these materials are quite difficult to model. Since the walls are protected by fire blankets covered by silver film, the walls are assumed well insulated and are modeled as adiabatic boundary conditions. This treatment is somewhat unrealistic and may result in faster fire spread. However, given the uncertainties and complications involved in performing any other treatments, this appears to be expedient. Second, the heat losses through the glass panel may be substantial. Although conduction loss is simulated, the radiative loss due to its transparency is not easily handled. Third, the chipboard properties used in the simulation

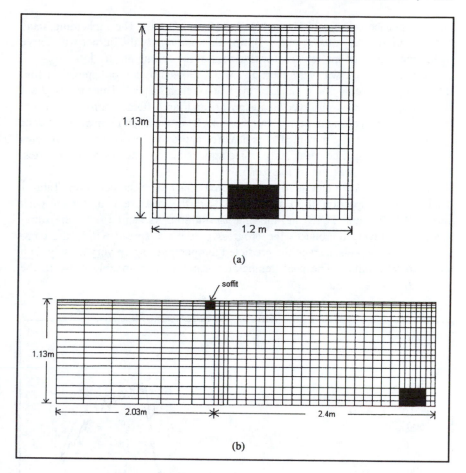

Figure 5. The flow domain computational mesh used in the simulation.
(a) The mesh in the xy plane. (b) The mesh in the yz plane.
The black regions in (a) and (b) represent the burner position.

are found from the literature. They may be not suitable to the particular material used in the test.

4. RESULTS AND DISCUSSIONS

The fire spread within the test compartment progressed through four distinct stages—preheating, ignition and rapid spread, fully developed, and finally decay. The process of fire spread in the compartment may be represented by the history of the upper layer temperature as measured by the two thermocouples suspended just beneath the ceiling, TCH1 and TCH2 (see Figure 6). The preheating stage lasted approximately nine minutes. During this phase only the burner was active within the compartment, with no involvement of the ceiling material.

The ignition stage was very short and was followed by a rapid spread of fire. It took approximately one minute for the fire to reach its peak. During this phase the compartment was observed to flashover, and large flames compared to the scale of the compartment were seen emerging from the open compartment door (see Figure 7). The fire remained at its peak for approximately one to two minutes and began to decay. The decay stage lasted approximately one and a half minutes. The total test time was almost fourteen minutes.

Figure 6 depicts the measured and predicted upper layer temperatures. Table 1 displays the comparison of the predictions with the measurements for the peak values of TCH1 and TCH2 and the time to ignition. As can be seen, the simulation qualitatively reproduces the progress of the fire spread within the compartment. In the preheat stage the predicted temperatures agree very closely with the measured values. The peak temperatures are also reasonably close to the

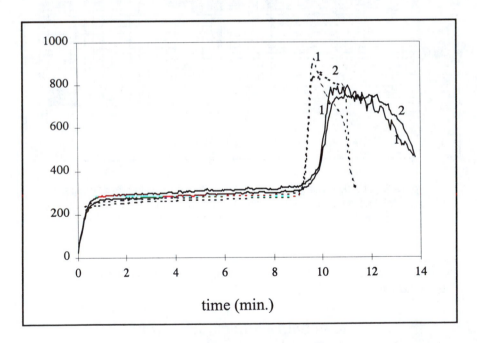

Figure 6. The predicted and measured temperatures (°C) as a function of time (min) at measuring locations defined by thermocouples TCH1 and TCH2 in the upper layer. 1: temperatures at TCH1 position; 2: temperatures at TCH2 position. solid: measured; broken line: predicted.

Figure 7. Photograph of test 4 taken at the moment the peak
temperatures were recorded.

measured peak values. In addition, the predicted time to ignite the chipboard agrees very well with the experimental observation.

For the first 11.5 minutes, the experimental measurements suggest that temperatures measured by TCH2 are lower than those measured by TCH1. This is consistent with the relative locations of the thermocouples, with TCH2 being located further away from the gas burner and the point where the fire first takes hold of the ceiling material. However, as the fire spreads forward along the ceiling, temperatures measured by TCH2 increase, and eventually exceed those measured by TCH1. In addition, temperatures at TCH2 remain at their peak value longer than those at TCH1. While these trends are reproduced by the numerical prediction, the simulated fire appears to spread more rapidly than the real fire. Furthermore, the simulated fire appears to decay earlier and more rapidly than the real fire. During the decay phase, both the experiment and the numerical prediction indicate that temperatures measured at TCH1 decrease more rapidly than TCH2.

The curves in Figure 8 represent the measured and predicted temperatures at the locations of TCLW1 to TCLW4. The peak values of TCLW1-TCLW4 are presented in Table 2. These thermocouples are located close to the left wall of the compartment. The shapes of the predicted temperature curves are similar to those of the measured temperature curves. In addition, the predicted peak temperatures at thermocouple locations TCLW2 and TCLW4 are in reasonably good agreement with the measured peak temperatures. Once again however, the predicted temperature curves indicate an early and more rapid decay of the simulated fire. Furthermore, the peak values of the predicted temperatures for TCLW1 and TCLW3 are considerably lower than those of the corresponding measured temperatures. It is thought that the location of these thermocouples may have contributed to this discrepancy. These thermocouples are located 0.6 m above the

Table 1. The Time to Ignition and Peak Temperatures at Thermocouple
Locations TCH1 and TCH2

	Measurements	Predictions
Approximate time to ignition	9.6 min	9.2 min
Approximate peak temperature of TCH1	800°C	910°C
Approximate peak temperature of TCH2	750°C	850°C

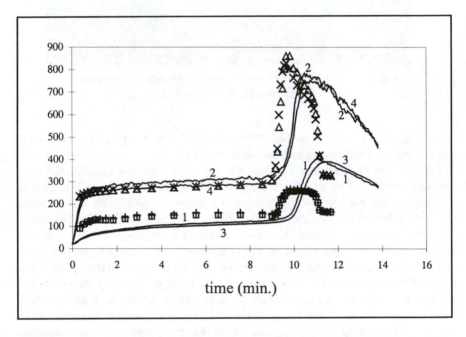

Figure 8. The predicted and measured temperatures (°C) as a function
of time (min) at the positions of TCLW1 to TCLW4.
2: TCLW2; 1: TCLW1; 4: TCLW4; 3: TCLW3.
solid: measured; broken: predicted.

floor and are thus in the transition region between the lower cool layer and the
upper hot layer. Temperatures in this region are very sensitive to changes of
height. As a result, they are most likely to suffer from poor predictions.

The predicted and measured temperature profiles of the thermocouple
tree located near the front wall are plotted in Figure 9. The predictions are in
qualitative agreement with the experiment. As the walls are assumed adiabatic, in
the preheating stage, the numerical temperatures are higher than the measured.
After the chipboard is ignited, the predicted temperatures at the three higher
locations are higher than the experiment while at the two lower positions the

Table 2. Peak Values of Temperature Measured and Predicted
at Thermocouple Locations TCLW1-TCLW4

	Measured Temperatures (°C)	Predicted Temperatures (°C)
Approximate peak value of TCLW1	400	260
Approximate peak value of TCLW2	780	830
Approximate peak value of TCLW3	390	265
Approximate peak value of TCLW4	750	860

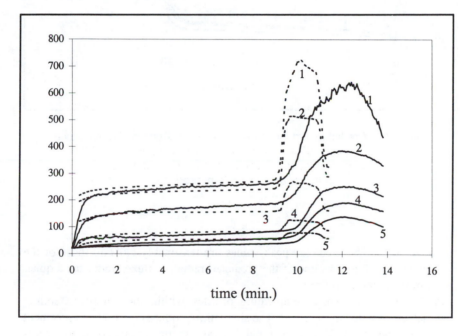

Figure 9. The predicted and measured temperatures (°C) as a function
of time (min) measured at locations TCT1 to TCT5.
1: 1.0m; 2: 0.8m; 3: 0.6m; 4: 0.4m; 5: 0.2m
solid: measured; broken: predicted.

temperatures are under predicted. As the simulated fire spreads more rapidly and
decays more quickly than the actual fire, the peaks of the predicted temperature
profiles shift backwards in time, i.e., occur earlier.

The curves of the measured and predicted radiative fluxes are drawn in
Figure 10. Good qualitative agreement with the experiment is achieved for

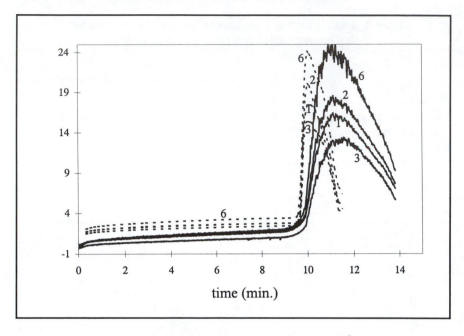

Figure 10. Predicted and measured radiative flux (kW/m^2) curves as a
function of time (min) for the six radiometers.
6: rad6; 2: rad2; 1: rad1; 5: rad5; 4: rad4; 3: rad3
solid: measured; broken: predicted.

the predictions. The predicted peak values are reasonably close to those of the measurements. Rapid decline of the predicted radiative fluxes indicates a quick decay of the simulation fire.

Predicted and measured temperature profiles within the chipboard ceiling material are depicted in Figure 11. The simulation produces qualitative agreement with the experiment. The more rapid increase in the predicted temperatures within the chipboard once again indicates that the simulated fire spreads more rapidly.

The shorter duration of the simulated fire can be explained as a result of its more rapid progress. The char layer formed as the chipboard is burning protects the virgin material from further pyrolysis. As a result, there is a rapid decline in the mass loss rate of the charring material after it reaches its peak. The more rapidly the fire spreads, the faster the rate at which the chipboard surface area is covered with a layer of char, resulting in a more rapid decline of the mass loss rate from the entire chipboard. Consequently, the simulated fire decays more rapidly than the real one.

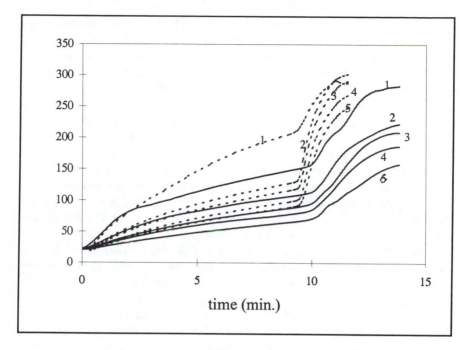

Figure 11. The predicted and measured temperatures (°C) as a function of
time (min) measured at locations TCW1 to TCW6.
1: TCW1; 2: TCW2; 3: TCW3; 4: TCW4; 5: TCW5; 6: TCW6.
solid: measured; broken: predicted.

In summary, good qualitative agreement between experiment and predictions
are achieved. In addition, some reasonable quantitative agreements between the
simulation and the experiment are obtained, for example, the peak values of the
upper layer temperatures and the radiative heat flux. Prior to the ceiling material
being involved in the combustion, quite good quantitative agreement between
predictions and experiment are produced. The predicted time to the involvement of the ceiling material is also in very good agreement with that measured.
However, the simulated fire spread more rapidly than the experimental fire
and consequently, the duration of the simulated fire spread is much shorter than
that measured.

These differences may have resulted from the nature of the model assumptions.
For example, the model does not take into account moisture within the fuel.
Moisture within the wood fuel may substantially reduce the heat release rate
when the wood is burned. Another key assumption concerns the imposition of
a constant pyrolysis temperature. Measurements suggest that the pyrolysis
temperature is dependent on the external heat flux (i.e., the greater the external

flux, the higher the resulting pyrolysis temperature). High pyrolysis temperature may significantly decrease the mass loss rate of the solid fuel since more surface re-radiation heat losses occur. Another plausible explanation for the differences between the numerical and experimental results concerns the use of improper char properties. This may result in the char layer being unable to provide sufficient insulation to the virgin material resulting in higher mass loss rates. Char properties may also vary with temperature. In addition, the secondary reactions of the combustible gases when going through the hot char layer change the composition of the volatiles and may thus reduce the heat release rate of the combustible gases. Finally, uncertainties in the basic material properties of the compartment building materials may also contribute to the observed differences.

It is worth noting that the simulation was also attempted using the six-flux radiation model in place of the discrete transfer radiation model. The attraction of the six-flux model is that it is more computational efficient in that it consumes considerably less computational power than the discrete transfer model. In these calculations, the six-flux model required twenty-six minutes compared with the discrete transfer models ninety minutes to perform ten time steps with 100 iterations in each time step on a 400 MHz DEC alpha workstation.

However, in using the six-flux model, the simulations failed to predict the fire spread within the fire compartment. Although the burning in the region directly above the burner was produced, the simulated fire was not able to spread out of that region. This may at first appear somewhat surprising as the six-flux radiation model was successful used in previous simulations incorporating solid phase combustion [14]. However, these cases made use of the non-charring pyrolysis model.

The current case included charring which creates a much more difficult fire spread situation. Furthermore, a more accurate prediction of the incident heat flux at the ceiling is required for the current case as a much larger span of target material is used here compared with the situation in reference 14, where only a small square sample of non-charring material was involved. In addition, the incident heat flux at the ceiling in the region normal to the burner is generally overestimated by the six-flux model, causing a faster growth of the insulation layer—the char layer which protects the material from further burning. Consequently, the mass loss rates in the mentioned region plummet. However, burning in this region is crucial for the simulated fire spreading during the earliest stage of fire spread. This would suggest that under these conditions, the six-flux radiation model should not be used.

5. CONCLUSIONS

This chapter concerned the development and demonstration of a fire field model intended to simulate the spread of fire within a compartment involving solid fuels. The fire model incorporated a gas-phase combustion model, a thermal radiation model that included the effect of soot, and a charring pyrolysis model, all within the context of a CFD-based fire field model. Particular attention was paid to express the interplay between the gas-phase and the solid-phase behaviors. This interplay can be represented by the boundary conditions at the surface of the solid material.

The three-dimensional fire spread model was used to simulate a fire test within a half-scale fire compartment. The ceiling of the test compartment was lined with chipboard, a material that chars when exposed to fire. The model produced predictions that were in good qualitative agreement with the experimental data. Some quantitative agreement between numerical and experimental data was also achieved, in particular the peak values of the upper layer temperatures and radiation fluxes. In addition, the simulation was able to produce good agreement with the experimental observations during the growth stage of the fire, and the model was able to predict to reasonable accuracy when the ceiling material became involved in the fire. However, the simulated fire spread more rapidly than the real fire. Consequently the duration of the simulated fire spread is much shorter than that of the real fire. These differences may result from the nature of some of the model assumptions. For example, the model ignores the moisture content of the wood fuel, assumes a constant pyrolysis temperature, lacks detailed thermal properties of the char, assumes that the char thermal properties are temperature independent and finally assumes values for the thermal properties of the compartment wall materials.

It was noted during the course of these investigations that the six-flux radiation model was not suitable for applications involving the spread of fire along a large expanse of combustible solid material that chars. In order to capture this behavior, it is necessary to incorporate a discrete transfer radiation model utilizing some fifty rays. While this incurs a significant computational overhead, the alternative approach using the six-flux model is unable to simulate the spread of the combustion front.

While the charring pyrolysis model adopted here appears to provide a promising approach to the prediction of fire spread within enclosures, much work remains before it can be applied to engineering applications of fire field modeling. The models reliance on simple treatment of gaseous combustion must be further assessed through, for example, the inclusion of ignition and extinction mechanisms for gaseous combustion. The model must also be further developed to include physical behavior such as downward flame spread, the inclusion of moisture in the solid fuel and an improved soot model. The models suitability for other fuels must also be established. A mechanism for predicting the generation of major toxic fire products such as CO should also be developed. Furthermore, additional quantitative validation of the model with experimental data must be performed. Work along all these lines is currently underway.

REFERENCES

1. E. R. Galea, On the Field Modelling Approach to the Simulation of Enclosure Fires, *Journal of Fire Protection Engineering, 1,* pp. 11-22, 1989.
2. S. Simcox, N. S. Wilkes, and I. P. Jones, Computer Simulation of the Flows of Hot Gases from the Fire at King's Cross Underground Station, *Fire Safety Journal, 18,* pp. 49-73, 1992.
3. E. R. Galea and N. C. Markatos, The Mathematical Modelling and Computer Simulation of Fire Development in Aircraft, *International Journal of Heat Mass Transfer, 34,* pp. 181-197, 1991.
4. N. C. Markatos and G. Cox, Hydrodynamics and Heat Transfer in Enclosures, *Physico-Chemical Hydrodynamics, 5,* pp. 53-66, 1984.
5. N. C. Markatos, M. R. Malin, and G. Cox, Mathematical Modelling of Buoyancy Induced Smoke Flow in Enclosures, *International Journal of Heat Mass Transfer, 25,* p. 63, 1982.
6. E. R. Galea, N. Hoffmann, and D. Berhane, Large-Scale Fire Field Modelling—The Route to General use via Parallel Processing, *Interflam '93,* Interscience, pp. 307-319, 1993.
7. E. R. Galea, D. Berhane, and N. A. Hoffmann, CFD Analysis of Fire Plumes Emerging from Windows with External Protrusions in High-Rise Buildings, *Proceedings Interflam '96,* compiled by C. Franks and S. Grayson, ISBN 0 9516320 9 4, pp. 835-839, 1996.
8. S. Kumar, A. K. Gupta, and G. Cox, Effects of Thermal Radiation on the Fluid Dynamics of Compartment Fires, *Fire Safety Science—Proceedings of the 3rd International Symposium,* pp. 345-354, 1991.
9. B. Karlsson, *Modeling Fire Growth on Combustible Lining Materials in Enclosures,* 992, Report TVBB-1009, Lund University, Department of Fire Safety Engineering, Lund, Sweden, 1992.
10. M. Luo and V. Beck, Flashover Fires in a Full Scale Building: Prediction and Experiment, *Proceedings Interflam '96,* compiled by C. Franks and S. Grayson, ISBN 0 9516320 9 4, pp. 361-370, 1996.
11. K. Opstad, *Modelling of Thermal Flame Spread on Solid Surfaces in Large-Scale Fires,* MTF-Report 1995:114(D), Department of Applied Mechanics, Thermo- and Fluid Dynamics, The Norwegian Institute of Technology, University of Trondheim, 1995.
12. F. Jia, E. R. Galea, and M. K. Patel, The Prediction of Fire Propagation in Enclosure Fires, *Proceedings of 5th International Symposium IAFSS,* Melbourne, Australia, pp. 439-450, 1997.
13. F. Jia, E. R. Galea, and K. M. Patel, Simulating "FLASHOVER" and "BACKDRAFT" Type Events Using Fire Field Models—A First Approximation, *Journal of Fire Protection Engineering, 9:4,* 1999.
14. F. Jia, E. R. Galea, and K. M. Patel, The Numerical Simulation of the Non-Charring Pyrolysis Process and Fire Development within a Compartment, *Applied Mathematical Modelling, 23,* pp. 587-607, 1999.
15. Z. Yan and G. Holmstedt, CFD and Experimental Studies of Room Fire Growth on Wall Lining Materials, *Fire Safety Journal, 27,* pp. 201-238, 1996.

16. F. Jia, E. R. Galea, and K. M. Patel, Numerical Simulation of the Mass Loss Process in Pyrolizing Char Materials, *Fire and Materials, 23,* pp. 71-78, 1999.
17. Y. Chen, M. A. Delichatsios, and V. Motevalli, Material Pyrolysis Properties, Part 1: An Integral Model for One Dimensional Transient Pyrolysis of Charring and Non-Charring Materials, *Combustion Science Technology, 88,* pp. 309-328, 1993.
18. B. Moghtaderi, V. Novozhilov, D. Fletcher, and J. H. Kent, An Integral Model for the Transient Pyrolysis of Solid Materials, *Fire and Materials, 21,* pp. 7-16, 1997.
19. A. D. Burns and N. S. Wilkes, *A Finite-Difference Method for the Computation of Fluid Flows in Complex Three Dimensional Geometries,* U.K. Atomic Energy Authority Harwell Report, AERE-R 12342, 1987.
20. F. Jia, *Simulations of Fire Growth and Spread Within Enclosures Using an Integrated CFD Fire Spread Model,* Ph.D. thesis, University of Greenwich, 1999.
21. B. Magnussen and B. H. Hjertager, On Mathematical Modelling of Turbulent Combustion with Special Emphasis on Soot Formation and Combustion, *16th International Symposium on Combustion,* The Combustion Institute, pp. 719-729, 1977.
22. J. B. Moss, C. D. Stewart, and K. J. Syed, Flowfield Modelling of Soot Formation at Elevated Pressure, *22nd International Symposium on Combustion,* pp. 413-423, 1988.
23. D. R. Honnery, M. Tappe, and J. H. Kent, Two Parametric models of Soot Growth Rates in Laminar Ethylene Diffusion Flames, *Combustion Science and Technology, 83,* pp. 305-321, 1992.
24. J. P. Gore and G. M. Faeth, Structure and Radiation Properties of Luminous Turbulent Acetylene/Air Diffusion Flames, *Journal of Heat Transfer, 110,* pp. 173-181, 1988.
25. M. Fairweather, W. P. Jones, and R. P. Lindstedt, Predictions of Radiative Transfer from a turbulent Reacting Jet in a Cross-Wind, *Combustion Flame, 89,* pp. 45-63, 1992.
26. N. Hoffman and N. C. Markatos, Thremal Radiation Effects on Fires in Enclosures, *Applied Mathematical Modelling, 12,* pp. 129-140, 1988.
27. F. C. Lockwood and N. G. Shah, A New Radiation Solution Method for Incorporation in General Combustion Prediction Procedures, *18th International Symposium on Combustion,* The Combustion Institute, pp. 1405-1414, 1981.
28. C. D. Blasi, Modelling and Simulation of Combustion Processes of Charring and Noncharring Solid Fuels, *Progress Energy Combustion Science, 19,* pp. 71-104, 1993.
29. T. Kashiwagi, Polymer Combustion and Flammability—Role of the Condensed Phase, *25th International Symposium on Combustion,* The Combustion Institute, p. 1423, 1994.
30. J. E. J. Staggs and R. H. Whiteley, Modelling the Combustion of Solid-Phase Fuels in Cone Calorimeter Experiments, *Proceedings Interflam '96,* compiled by C. Franks and S. Grayson, ISBN 0 9516320 9 4, pp. 103-112, 1996.
31. M. M. Delichatsios, M. K. Mathews, and M. A. Delichatsios, An Upward Fire Spread and Growth Simulation, *Fire Safety Science—Proceedings of the Third International Symposium,* pp. 207-216, 1991.
32. D. Hopkins, Jr. and J. G. Quintiere, Material Fire Properties and Predictions for Thermoplastics, *Fire Safety Journal, 26,* pp. 241-268, 1996.
33. M. N. Özisik, *Heat Conduction,* John Wiley & Sons, Inc., New York, 1980.

34. Lockwood, F. C. and M. G. Malalasekera, Fire Computation: The Flashover Phenomenon, *22nd International Symposium on Combustion,* The Combustion Institute, pp. 1319-1328, 1988.
35. W. W. Yuen and C. L. Tien, A Simple Calculation Scheme for the Luminous Flame Emissivity, *16th International Symposium on Combustion,* pp. 1481-1487, 1977.
36. G. L. Hubbard and C. L. Tien, Infrared Mean Absorption Coefficients of Luminous Flames and Smoke, *Journal of Heat Transfer, 100,* pp. 235-239, 1978.
37. M. A. Delichatsios and Y. Chen, Flame Spread on Charring Materials: Numerical Predictions and Critical Conditions, *Fire Safety Science—Proceedings of the 4th International Symposium,* pp. 457-468, 1994.

CHAPTER 8

Numerical Modeling of Radiative Heat Transfer in Integrated CFD Fire Modeling

E. P. Keramida, N. N. Souris, A. G. Boudouvis, and N. C. Markatos

Thermal radiation, although considered an important mode of heat transfer in high temperature conditions, is often neglected in fire modeling, mainly due to the complex physics involved. The aim of this study is to provide modelers with guidance on the engineering treatment of radiation transfer; two widely used radiation models are reviewed and their performance is assessed in a benchmark experimental enclosure fire case. The discrete transfer and the six-flux radiation models are compared in terms of computational efficiency, ease of application, and predictive accuracy. The predictions are evaluated as part of a complete prediction procedure involving the modeling of the simultaneously occurring flow, convection, and radiation phenomena. The results have demonstrated that the effect of thermal radiation is important, even in small fires. Comparison between the two models indicates that the simple six-flux model suffices for small compartment fires, up to 100 kW.

Thermal radiation can be an important mode of heat transfer in processes involving high temperatures and for that reason the computational analysis of thermal radiation transfer in enclosure fire modeling is essential. Predicting possible secondary ignition, for example, due to thermal radiation is particularly important in fire safety engineering. Another case in point is the blocking of radiant heat by a water spray or mist, as an important mechanism in fire extinguishment. Radiation modeling is difficult because it involves complex mathematics, increased computation times, and significant uncertainty concerning the optical properties of the participating media and surfaces. However, ignoring radiative transfer may introduce significant errors in the overall predictions.

Most of the major developments in the engineering treatment of radiative transfer have been driven by the need for accurate predictions in industrial furnaces. Consequently, there have been numerous evaluations of radiation models for furnaces. For fire modeling, on the other hand, very few have been undertaken. Utilizing the methods developed for furnace applications is common practice in fire engineering. However, when applied to enclosure fire simulations, the performance of these models is expected to differ, as the physical processes and the time and length scales considered are of different order of magnitude, compared to those in furnaces. The ratio of the combustion area to the overall configuration volume, is an example; in furnaces the ratio ranges between 1:1 and 1:2, while in compartment fires it ranges between 1:10 and 1:100. Another example is the steeper temperature gradients that are observed in a fire environment, which affect the radiative heat exchange rates. Moreover, unlike furnaces, where attention is focused inside the flame, in compartment fires investigation is extended in locations away from the flame (upper layer, door jets, etc.) Finally, combustion furnaces are two-dimensional, while compartment fires are of less homogeneity, three-dimensional problems. Those specific requirements are distinguishing fires from the very extensive investigations already undertaken in the radiation heat transfer field, making prior examination and justification of model choice necessary.

This chapter describes the application and the performance of two radiation models in CFD calculations for the simulation of thermal radiation transfer in a fire induced flow in a domestic sized room.

RADIATION MODELING

There are several analytical methods presently used for the engineering treatment of radiative heat transfer in participating media. The most accurate ones are considered to be the zone and the Monte Carlo methods [see 1 for an extensive review]. However, these methods are not widely used in comprehensive combustion calculations due to their large computational time and storage requirements. Additionally, the above-mentioned models are in non-differential form, providing a significant inconvenience in solving them simultaneously with the remaining equations of fluid flow.

Modeling of the simultaneously occurring flow, chemical reaction, and heat transfer in a transient fire atmosphere involving more than one phase, can be a CPU demanding procedure with respect to computer time. As economy is particularly important in the development of fire simulation codes, the radiation model used should not only be realistic enough to yield meaningful predictions, but also simple and fast enough to avoid excessive overall computational cost.

One such model is the six-flux model of Schuster and Hamaker, as formulated by Spalding [2]. It's easy to understand, readily applicable, and fast, but of limited accuracy, and has successfully been applied to a number of fire cases

[3-5]. On the other hand, the discrete transfer model of Lockwood and Shah [6], has received much attention in the engineering treatment of fire radiation during the last decade [see 7-10 for example]; combining features of the zone, Monte Carlo and the flux models, is considered a more fundamental and accurate model.

These two models are applied here to an experimental benchmark fire case in an attempt to evaluate them in terms of computational efficiency, ease of application, and predictive accuracy. The strengths and limitations of the two models are discussed in more detail below.

With the discrete transfer model, the total radiative flux is calculated by integrating the energy contribution along rays emanating from the radiative source and pointing in any selected direction.

The advantages of the discrete transfer model are:

1. retains the physics of the problem using relatively simple mathematics;
2. has the ability to return any desired degree of accuracy by increasing the number of rays projected from each physical surface and the number of zones that the domain is divided into, adding of course, considerably to the cost of computation;

The disadvantages of the discrete transfer model are:

1. requires a surface model to describe the geometry;
2. requires carefully shaped control volumes and positioning of the rays to yield accurate predictions.

The six-flux method accounts for contributions to the radiative flux coming from only six directions, parallel and anti-parallel to the three coordinate directions. It is a differential model providing convenience in the discretization of the transport equations.

The advantages of the six-flux model are:

1. retains the important effects relevant to fire scenarios, although it assumes that radiation is transmitted in coordinate directions only;
2. offers computational economy;
3. solves directly on the flow spatial grid, needs no special description of the geometry;

The disadvantages of the six-flux model are:

1. has no inter-linkages, apart from scattering, between the radiation fluxes in the respective coordinate directions;
2. is quite accurate for optically thick media, but it will yield inaccurate results for thinner (transparent) media, especially near boundaries, and also if the radiation field is anisotropic;
3. fails in cases of complex geometry, such as congested spaces, or many and large openings.

THE PHYSICAL AND MATHEMATICAL MODEL

Compartment Configuration

The case simulated draws from an experiment conducted by Steckler et al. [11] to investigate fire induced flows in a compartment measuring 2.8 m × 2.8 m in plane and 2.18 m in height, containing a constant fire of 62.9 kW. The walls were 0.1 m thick and the walls and ceiling were covered with a light ceramic fiber insulation board. A two-dimensional array of bi-rectional velocity probes and bare-wire thermocouples was placed in a vertical plane located midway between the inner and outer edges of the door jamb. In this way temperatures and velocities could be measured throughout the doorway across its width and through its height. In addition, a stack of aspirated thermocouples were placed in the front corner of the room to measure the gas temperature profile.

This is a well studied case, used many times in previous works for validation [4, 12, 13]. A number of simulations are performed based on three fire locations (Figure 1), three door widths—0.24, 0.74 and 0.99 m, and one fire size—62.9 kW. The door openings used in these simulations measured 1.83 m in height.

Mathematical Model

A three-dimensional mathematical model is used to simulate the flow in the chamber. The model consists of the partial differential equations describing the conservation of momentum, heat transfer, and mass species, in conjunction with a two-equation turbulence model. The precise formulation of the differential equations describing the model will not be given here as they may be found elsewhere [14, 15]. The turbulence kinetic energy and the dissipation of turbulence are calculated with the k-ε model, with buoyancy modifications [16]. Compressibility is accounted for by the ideal gas equation of state. The heat release of the fire is distributed in space accordingly to the Heskestad relation [17], $l = 0.23Q - 1.02D$, where l, is the plume height, Q, is the heat flux generated by fire, and D, is the diameter of surface area of fire.

The initial temperature was set to the measured ambient value while the walls of the compartment were modeled with the no-slip conditions for the velocities and isothermal conditions for the temperature. In order to correctly model the flow through the open door, the numerical grid was extended by 1.4 m to include a region outside the fire compartment. A fixed pressure boundary condition was used on all external boundaries. The solution domain is modeled using a mesh of 26880 cells. The mesh consisted of thirty-two cells in length, twenty-eight cells in width, and thirty cells in height. The mesh was non-uniformly distributed with refinements in the wall, floor, ceiling, fire, and doorway regions.

The problem was run in transient mode, typically requiring 200 time steps before reaching steady-state conditions. Within each time step, convergence was

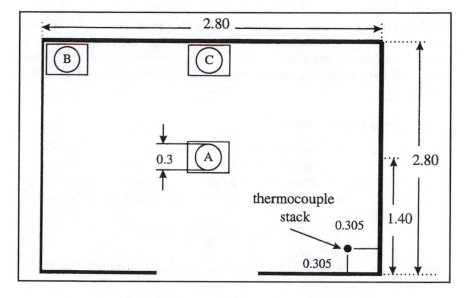

Figure 1. Layout of the compartment showing the location of three fire sources used in the simulations.

assumed if the mass source residual fell below $1 \times 10^{-0.4}$ (and the other key residual measures, e.g., enthalpy fell by the corresponding amounts). If the time step iteration was not stopped by these measures then a maximum of 100 iterations would be achieved when the maximum change between spot values fell to less than 1 percent between time steps.

The resulting system of the partial differential equations for the various dependent variables, along with the boundary and inlet conditions is solved using Cartesian coordinates and an iterative procedure, based on a staggered grid arrangement, using the hybrid differencing discretization scheme and the Stone method. The pressure-correction equation was solved using the conjugate gradient method and the turbulence quantities were solved using a line method. A fully implicit backward differencing scheme was used for the time discretization. A general purpose CFD commercial package, the CFX4.1, was used for the present work.

Radiation Models

The basis of all methods for the solution of radiation problems is the radiative transfer equation (RTE) [18]:

$$\underline{s} \cdot \nabla I(\underline{r},\underline{s}) = -\kappa(\underline{r})I(\underline{r},\underline{s}) + Q(\underline{r},\underline{s}) \tag{1}$$

which describes the radiative intensity field, I, within the enclosure, as a function of location vector ($\underline{r}$) and direction vector ($\underline{s}$); Q represents the total attenuation of the radiative intensity due to the gas emission and to the in-scattered energy from other directions to the direction of propagation, and κ is the total extinction coefficient.

The Discrete Transfer Model

The discrete transfer model discretizes the RTE along rays. The path along a ray is discretized by using the sections formed by breaking the path at zone boundaries. Assuming that the physical properties remain constant inside a zone, equation (1) can be integrated from zone entry to zone exit (Figure 2) to yield:

$$I_{n+1} = I_n e^{-\tau_n} + L_n Q_n \left[\frac{1 - e^{\tau_n}}{\tau_n} \right]; \tau_n = \kappa L_n \tag{2}$$

where L_n is the path length in the nth zone, I_n and I_{n+1} are the intensities at zone entry and zone exit respectively, and

$$Q_n(\underline{r},\underline{s}) = \frac{k_a}{\pi} \sigma T_n^4 + k_s J_n(\underline{r}) \tag{3}$$

where k_a, k_s, are the absorption and scattering coefficients for a gray medium, $J_n(\underline{r}) = \frac{1}{4n} \int I_n(\underline{r},\underline{s}) d\Omega$ is the mean intensity of the in-scattered radiation, σ is the Stefan-Boltzmann constant and $d\Omega$ is the element of solid angle containing $\underline{s}$.

The Six-Flux Model

The model employs diffusion-type differential equations for calculating radiative heat transfer. The solid angle surrounding a point is divided into six solid angles. The following second-order ordinary differential equations describe in Cartesian coordinates the six-flux model:

$$\frac{d}{dx} \left[\frac{l}{k_s + k_a)} \frac{d(RX)}{dx} \right] = (k_s + k_a) RX - k_a \sigma T^4 - \frac{k_s}{3} (RX + RY + RZ) \tag{4}$$

RX, RY, and RZ (W/m^2) are the composite radiative fluxes in x-, y-, and z-directions, respectively, σ is the Stefan-Boltzmann constant, 5.6678×10^{-8} (Wm^{-2}K^{-4}). Each of the differential flux equations expresses the attenuation of a flux with distance as a result of absorption and scattering and its augmentation by emission and scattering from other directions.

COMPUTATIONAL DETAILS

The absorption coefficient of the smoke is defined as [18],

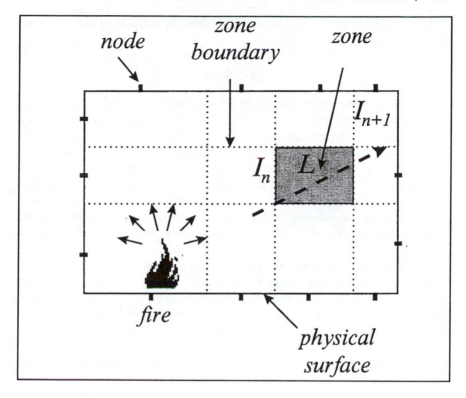

Figure 2. Sub-division of the solution domain into zones.

$$k_{a,s} = \kappa T f_v \qquad (5)$$

where f_v, is the smoke volume fraction, T (K), is the smoke temperature, which is here assumed to be equal to the gas temperature, and $\kappa = 1266\ K^{-1}m^{-1}$, is a constant dependent on the soot index of refraction, $m = n + ki$, resulting from the composition of the soot (here taken as $m = 1.57 + 0.56i$ [19]). Scattering by the smoke particles is neglected, assuming that they were very small. The walls were assumed infinitely thin, treated as gray heat sinks of emissivity 0.9, and the temperatures were set to ambient values, due to lack of any other experimental data [4, 12, 13]. It is noted in previous works that the wall boundary conditions have a great influence in the results of the simulations [see 4 for an extensive review]. A few degrees variation may result to a significant change of the total heat losses of the system, and that is why a full treatment utilizing wall material properties would be more realistic.

As already mentioned, the discrete transfer model may yield any desired degree of precision by increasing the number of rays and the number of zones. Results with various numbers of rays have been obtained, demonstrating that thirty-two rays suffice for accurate predictions.

RESULTS

Comparisons between the experimental data reported by Steckler et al. [11] and the calculated results obtained with and without radiation are shown in Figures 3 through 9. Door center vertical velocity and temperature profiles and corner stack vertical temperature profiles, for two door widths—0.24 and 0.74 m, and two fire locations—in the center and in the corner of the room are presented. As already mentioned by Kerrison et al. [12], temperatures are over-predicted by as much as 25 percent when thermal radiation is not taken into account. It is shown here, that accounting for radiation in the computational analysis, by either of the methods, has substantially improved the agreement between predictions and measurements.

The reduction of the mean temperature in the hot upper layer is significant and is more pronounced in the case where the fire is located in the corner (see Figures 6 through 8). The average upper layer temperature is higher and hence the effects of radiation are more significant for those cases in which the fire is located adjacent to the walls. The opposite trend is observed in the lower layer,

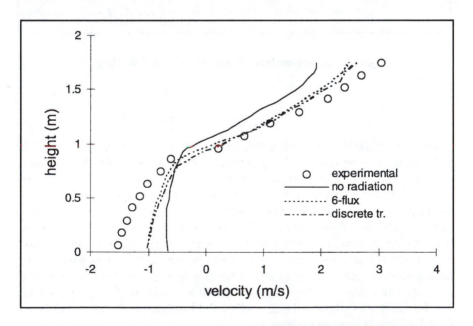

Figure 3. Numerical and experimental door center vertical velocity profiles for the 0.24 m wide door. The fire is located in the corner of the room.

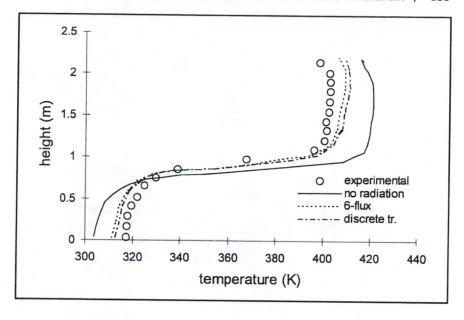

Figure 4. Numerical and experimental corner stack vertical temperature profiles for the 0.74 m wide door. The fire is located centrally.

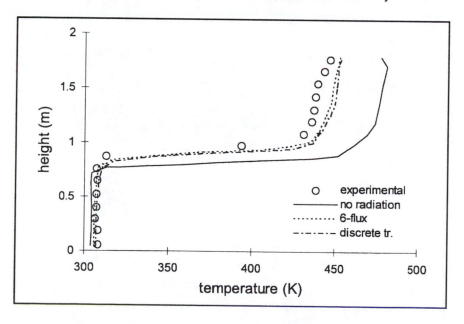

Figure 5. Numerical and experimental door center vertical temperature profiles for the 0.24 m wide door. The fire is located centrally.

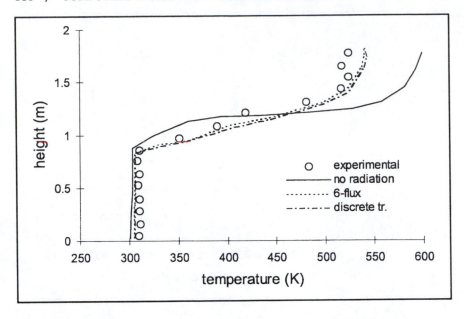

Figure 6. Numerical and experimental door center vertical temperature profiles for the 0.24 m wide door. The fire is located in the corner of the room.

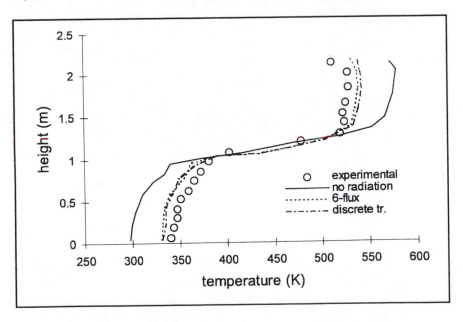

Figure 7. Numerical and experimental corner stack vertical temperature profiles for the 0.24 m wide door. The fire is located in the corner of the room.

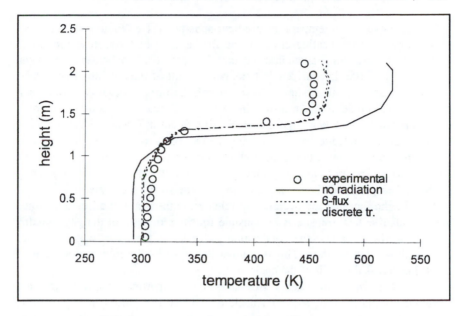

Figure 8. Numerical and experimental corner stack vertical temperature profiles for the 0.74 m wide door. The fire is located in the corner of the room.

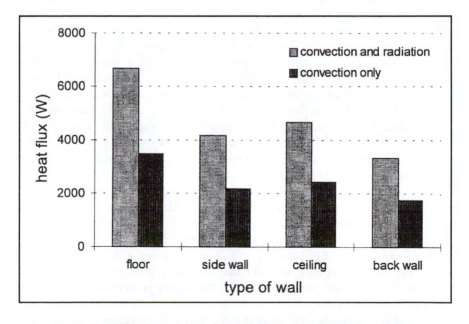

Figure 9. Heat fluxes across the walls of the compartment with and without radiation. The fire is located centrally.

where an elevation in temperature predictions is noted (see Figures 4, 7, and 8). This shows that the heating effect in the fire level is better represented, when radiation heat transfer is taken into account. This effect cannot be described when buoyant convection is considered alone, because all of the enthalpy released by the fire is pumped into the upper layer through the fire plume. It is obvious that this particular mode of heat transfer allows energy to reach any point of the room that can actually be "seen" by the fire. No significant differences were observed between the predicted temperatures using the two radiation models.

The position of the neutral plane, which is determined here by calculating the approximate location of the zero velocity line within the doorway, is also slightly affected, being shifted about 3 percent closer to the soffit (see Table 1).

Despite the fact that the overall heat released is the same in all the examined cases, radiative heat transfer is responsible for the reduction of the gas enthalpy content at the door jet—the combustion gases leave the room with nearly 15 percent lower temperature. This is counter-balanced by the increase of the total heat flux across the walls of the enclosure.

Figure 9 shows the total heat losses across the compartment walls, for the case where the fire is centrally located. Absolute wall heat flux values are significantly increased when radiation is taken into account. In this case the total heat flux from the wall is due to the sum of contributions of the convective and radiative heat transfer. The total heat leaving through the bounding surfaces is nearly doubled.

In terms of predictive accuracy the two radiation models have performed very similarly (see Figures 3 through 8). This confirms that the six-flux model, although crude in principle, is adequate for predicting the overall features of the flow in small fire cases. This is an important result, when it comes to simplified heat transfer analysis in fire simulations, given that the six-flux model is significantly simpler than the discrete transfer model regarding mathematics and implementation effort. It should be noted that this model offers a significant convenience for the engineer, that it can easily be incorporated in any 3-D CFD analysis by simply introducing three scalar transport equations into the calculations—describing the diffusive transfer of the three radiation fluxes—and by setting the corresponding boundary conditions.

The total CPU time requirements at Silicon Graphics Workstation, R4400 processor, 100 MHz were 32 h with the six-flux model and 44 h with the discrete transfer model. Concerning the implementation effort for the discrete transfer model, this is related to the fact that the model requires a geometrical description of its own to work. The construction of this geometry, which is based on surface modeling, requires carefully selected control volumes (zones) and positioning of the rays to achieve the required solution. The results produced by the discrete transfer model are sensitive to the zone construction. Crude or careless "zoning" of the heat source (flame) will result in inaccurate average values of the temperature per zone and consequently, to inaccurate radiation calculations. The reason

Table 1. Comparison of Predictions of Neutral Plane Height/
Door Height (N/H$_0$, Mass Flow Rates, and Average Upper-Layer
Temperature with Experimental Results

Scenario	N/H$_0$	Mass Flow Rate (kg/sec)		Average Hot Layer Temp (K)
		In	Out	
A, 0.24m, 62.9kW				
Numerical*	0.473	0.232	0.240	523
Numerical**	0.495	0.249	0.245	481
Experimental	0.499	0.255	0.247	463
A, 0.74m, 62.9kW				
Numerical*	0.490	0.609	0.610	427
Numerical**	0.539	0.578	0.587	412
Experimental	0.561	0.554	0.571	402
A, 0.99m, 62.9kW				
Numerical*	0.503	0.761	0.769	399
Numerical**	0.571	0.695	0.720	387
Experimental	0.582	0.653	0.701	382
B, 0.24m, 62.9kW				
Numerical*	0.578	0.161	0.163	560
Numerical**	0.536	0.181	0.187	532
Experimental	0.523	0.201	0.205	521
B, 0.74m, 62.9kW				
Numerical*	0.677	0.285	0.287	505
Numerical**	0.596	0.380	0.392	469
Experimental	0.566	0.435	0.462	454
B, 0.99m, 62.9kW				
Numerical*	0.697	0.298	0.299	481
Numerical**	0.603	0.459	0.446	456
Experimental	0.586	0.513	0.491	445
C, 0.74m, 62.9kW				
Numerical*	0.653	0.331	0.332	459
Numerical**	0.598	0.415	0.420	430
Experimental	0.579	0.474	0.476	425

*Without radiation
**With radiation (six-flux)

for that is that in large systems the spatial resolution (number of zones) is normally much less than that used by the flow solver. This mainly affects the cooling rate, which is proportional to the fourth power of the temperature and can thus change by several orders of magnitude across a flame front. Large local errors occur if large opacity gradients remain unresolved by the radiation model [20]. In Figure 10, case 1 is an example of crude zoning, while case 3 is an example of more careful zoning that takes into account the steep temperature variation from zone to zone. Another important issue when "zoning" the heat sources, is to ensure symmetry; comparison between case 2a and case 2b in Figure 10 shows the difference.

Finally, it must be noted that the above observations apply only for small volumetric heat release rates, up to 100 kW. The results of a preliminary study with bigger fires, (more than 100 kW fires), indicate that the accuracy of the six-flux model is uncertain, and for that reason the discrete transfer model should be used. On the other hand, the inclusion or not of gaseous combustion in the computations does not affect the above conclusions [see 21 for more details].

CONCLUSIONS

The present work investigates numerically a small fire induced flow in a room-sized compartment with and without consideration of the radiation effects. Two radiation models, namely the six-flux model and the discrete transfer model, have been used for this purpose.

The results have confirmed that the effect of thermal radiation is important even for small fire temperature predictions. The inclusion of radiative heat transfer in the fire analysis has produced a better agreement between the numerical predictions and the experimental data. It has resulted in an increase of the levels of computed temperatures near the floor, and in a substantial decrease in the hot upper layer, near the ceiling. These observations indicate that computations involving only convective heat transfer mechanisms under-estimate the heating effect of the air and the walls at the bottom half of the room, and over-predict the temperature levels everywhere else.

The inclusion of thermal radiation in the problem has also affected the neutral plane height. Finally, the results indicate that a significant percentage of the heat released by the fire, approximately 25 percent, is transferred through radiation toward the bounding surfaces of the system, where it is either absorbed or reflected. The percentage of heat leaving through the walls of the system is doubled, emphasizing the significance of this particular sink term in the total enthalpy balance analysis.

Finally, the two models have performed very similarly, both showing good agreement with the experimental data. This indicates that the modeler dealing with fires smaller than 100 kW can take advantage of the simplicity and lower computational requirements of the six-flux model and use it with relative ease

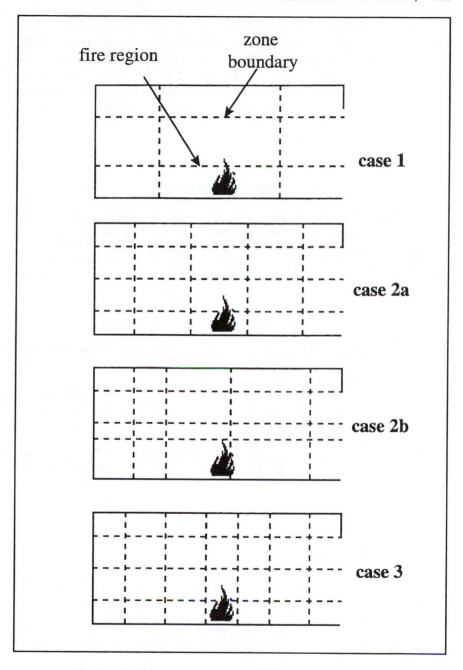

Figure 10. Hypothetical zone constructions, showing different sampling of the fire.

and confidence in describing the radiative heat transfer in a compartment fire. Moreover, the discrete transfer model, although it has shown an acceptable predictive accuracy, that is not sensitive to fire size, it possesses two important disadvantages that the modeler should be aware of: (1) it is not as easy to incorporate into fire codes, because it requires its own geometrical description, (2) it may prove tricky in terms of dividing the domain into zones to describe the geometry, and (3) is computationally more expensive (double the CPU time required by the six-flux procedure).

REFERENCES

1. J. R. Howell, Thermal Radiation in Participating Media: The Past, the Present, and Some Possible Futures, *ASME Journal of Heat Transfer, 110,* p. 1220, 1998.
2. A. D. Gosman, W. M. Pun, A K. Runchal, D. B. Spalding, and M. W. Wolfshtein, *Heat and Mass Transfer in Recirculating Flows,* Academic Press, New York, 1969.
3. N. Hoffmann and N. C. Markatos, Thermal Radiation Effects on Fires in Enclosures, *Applied Mathematical Modelling, 12,* pp. 129-140, 1988.
4. S. Kumar, A. K. Gupta, and G. Cox, Effects of Thermal Radiation on the Fluid Dynamics of Compartment Fires, *Third International Symposium on Fire Safety Science,* pp. 345-354, 1991.
5. F. Jia, E. R. Galea, and M. K. Patel, The Numerical Simulation of the Noncharring Pyrolysis Process and Fire Development within a Compartment, *Applied Mathematical Modelling, 23,* pp. 587-607, 1999.
6. F. C. Lockwood and N. G. Shah, A New Radiation Solution Method for Incorporation in General Combustion Prediction Procedures, *Proceedings of the Eighteenth Symposium (Inter.) on Combustion,* The Combustion Institute, Pittsburgh, pp. 1405-1416, 1981.
7. M. Luo, Y. He, and V. Beck, Application of Field Model and Two-Zone Model to Flashover Fires in a Full-Scale Multi-Room Single Level Building, *Fire Safety Journal, 29,* pp. 1-26, 1997.
8. Z. Yan and G. Holmstedt, CFD and Experimental Studies of Room Fire Growth on Wall Lining Materials, *Fire Safety Journal, 27,* pp. 201-238, 1996.
9. D. F Fletcher, J. H. Kent, V. B. Apte, and A. R. Green, Numerical Simulations of Smoke Movement from a Pool Fire in a Ventilated Tunnel, *Fire Safety Journal, 23,* pp. 305-325, 1994.
10. M. Luo and V. Beck, The Fire Environment in a Multi-Room Building—Comparison of Predicted and Experimental Results, *Fire Safety Journal, 23,* pp. 413-438, 1994.
11. K. D. Steckler, J. G. Quintiere, and W. J. Rinkinen, *Flow Induced by Fire in a Compartment,* U.S. Department of Commerce, NBSIR 82-2520, 1982.
12. L. Kerrison, E. R. Galea, N. Hoffmann, and M. K. Patel, A Comparison of a FLOW3D Based Fire Field Model with Experimental Room Fire Data, *Fire Safety Journal, 23,* pp. 387-411, 1994.
13. N. Fusegi, T. Toru, K. Farouk, and J. Bakhtier, Numerical Study on Interactions of Turbulent Convection and Radiation in Compartment Fires, *Fire Science and Technology, 8,* pp. 15-31, 1988.

14. N. C. Markatos and G. Cox, Hydrodynamics and Heat Transfer in Enclosures Containing a Fire Source, *Physicochemical Hydrodynamics, 5,* pp. 53-65, 1984.
15. E. R. Galea and N. C. Markatos, The Mathematical Modelling and Computer Simulation of Fire Development in Aircraft, *International Journal of Heat Mass Transfer, 34,* pp. 181-197, 1984.
16. N. C. Markatos, M. R. Malin, and G. Cox, Mathematical Modelling of Buoyancy-Induced Smoke Flow in Enclosures, *International Journal of Heat Mass Transfer, 25,* pp. 63-75, 1982.
17. G. Heskestad, Engineering Relations for Fire Plumes, *Fire Safety Journal, 7,* pp. 25-32, 1984.
18. M. F. Modest, *Radiative Heat Transfer,* McGraw Hill, New York, 1993.
19. C. Shaddix and K. Smyth, Laser-Induced Incandescence Measurements of Soot Production in Steady and Flickering Methane, Propane, and Ethylene Diffusion Flames, *Combustion and Flame, 107,* pp. 418-431, 1996.
20. E. P. Keramida, A N. Karayannis, A. G. Boudouvis, and N. C. Markatos, Radiative Heat Transfer in Fire Modeling, *NIST Annual Conference on Fire Research,* NISTIR 6242, Gaithersburg, pp. 147-149, 1998.
21. E. P. Keramida, H. H. Liakos, M. Founti, A. G. Boudouvis, and N. C. Markatos, Radiative Heat Transfer in Natural Gas-Fired Furnaces, *International Journal of Heat Mass Transfer, 43,* pp. 1801-1809, 2000.

Contributors

BEARD, ALAN, studied physics at Leicester University and in 1972 was awarded a Ph.D. in theoretical physics from Durham University for his thesis entitled *A calculation of Neutron-Deutron scattering using the SU(3) basis of three particle states*. On completion of his Ph.D., he conducted post-doctoral research in medical physics at Exeter University and the University of Wales, Dental School, Cardiff. In 1977 he started research in the Fire Safety Engineering Unit at Edinburgh University, leaving in 1995 to become a lecturer at Heriot-Watt University. He has acquired a wide knowledge of fire modeling and has conducted work for both government departments and industrial companies. He was instrumental in the establishment of a Home Office working group, the Fire Models Context Group, of which he is a member. The Group is concerned with the setting up of standards and a regulatory framework for the use of fire models. His papers have been used as key references by the International Standards Organization and some of his work has been translated into Japanese. He is also a member of the Fire Study Group of the Institution of Structural Engineers. For over 20 years Dr. Beard's research has centered around fire modeling. He has constructed both probabilistic and deterministic models of fire development. His previous work includes a six-year project on the probabilistic modeling of fire growth in hospital wards, funded by the Department of Health and the fore-runner of the Engineering and Physical Sciences Research Council (EPSRC).

BISHOP, STEVEN R., is an applied mathematician who, after his Ph.D., in 1989 was awarded a prestigious five year Advanced Research Fellowship from the UK Science and Engineering Research Council to consider the design implications of nonlinear dynamics for engineering systems. This period stimulated research projects in diverse areas covering ship capsize, impacting systems, control of chaos, chaotic synchronization as well as fire dynamics. Typically the mathematics content of each is similar and based on simple models to improve understanding of the underlying dynamical mechanisms. In 1991, together with Professor Michael Thompson FRS, he formed the Centre for Nonlinear Dynamics at University College London where he now holds the position of Centre Manager and Professor of Nonlinear Dynamics.

BOUDOUVIS, ANDREAS G., is an associate professor in the Chemical Engineering Department at the National Technical University of Athens (NTUA). He teaches fluid mechanics and computational methods. His research interests are in interfacial mechanics, magnetofluid mechanics, simulation of plasma processing, large-scale computing and nonlinear systems. He has co-authored over fifty publications in referred journals and international conference proceedings. Among other activities, he is a member of AIChE, SIAM, and the International Association for Hydromagnetic Phenomena and Applications. He holds a Diploma from NTUA (1982) and a Ph.D. from the University of Minnesota (1987), both in chemical engineering. Email: boudouvi@chemeng.ntua.gr.

CASCIATI, FABIO, received the Ph.D. in Civil Engineering in 1972. He has been a member of the faculty of the University of Pavia since 1974 now holding the rank of Full Professor of Structural Mechanics in the School of Engineering. From 1994 he has held the post of Coordinator of the Ph.D. Course in Civil Engineering. Dr. Casciati is a member of the Editorial Boards of Earthquake Engineering and Structural Dynamics, Structural Control, Structural Safety, Non-Linear Dynamics, Journal of Vibrations and Control, and Computer Aided Civil and Infrastructure Engineering. He is the author of Probabilistic Methods in Civil Engineering (co-authors G. Augusti and A. Baratta) and Fragility Analysis of Complex Structural Systems (co-author L. Faravelli). Fabio Casciati is author or co-author of more than 200 papers on structural reliability, stochastic mechanics, structural control, boundary element analysis and earthquake engineering. He is also coordinator of a number of European Union research projects.

DONEGAN, H. A., has been associated with research into firesafety engineering over the past fifteen years. He has concentrated his research on the modeling of building evacuations and on decision theory associated with firesafety evaluation. Dr. Donegan, a Chartered Engineer and Chartered Mathematician, is a Reader within the Mathematics Division of the Faculty of Informatics at the University of Ulster.

DRYSDALE, DOUGAL, studied Chemistry at the University of Edinburgh, and completed a Ph.D. in combustion chemistry at the University of Cambridge in 1966. He then spent time at the University of Toronto as a post-doctoral fellow, before joining the Department of Physical Chemistry at Leeds University where he worked on the evaluation of kinetic data for combustion and atmospheric processes. Since 1974, he has been at the University of Edinburgh, teaching

Fire Safety Engineering at postgraduate level between 1974 and 1986. In 1982, he spent a semester as Visiting Professor at the Centre for Firesafety Studies, Worcester Polytechnic Institute, Massachusetts where he prepared the first draft of his textbook "Introduction to Fire Dynamics," which was published in 1986. He has been editor of Fire Safety Journal since 1988, and in 1990 he was appointed Reader in Fire Safety Engineering in the Department of Civil and Environmental Engineering. He was elected European Vice-Chairman of the IAFSS in 1994, and was awarded the Arthur B. Guise Medal by the SFPE in 1995. His research interests lie in the fire properties of combustible materials, fire spread mechanisms, and fire dynamics. He was appointed to a Personal Chair in Fire Safety Engineering in 1998. The second edition of "Introduction to Fire Dynamics" was published by John Wiley and Sons in November 1998.

FARAVELLI, LUCIA, received the Ph.D. degree in Mathematics in 1972 and has served on the faculty of the University of Pavia from 1975 to 1990 and from 1991 to the present. From 1990 to 1991 she was Full Professor of Structural Mechanics at the School of Engineering at the University of Perugia. She is now Full Professor of Structural Safety, School of Engineering, University of Pavia and since 1995 has served as Dean of the School of Engineering at the same institution. She is Editor of the *Journal of Structural Control* and author and co-author of two books: *Sicurezza Strutturale* (in Italian), and *Fragility Analysis of Complex Structural Systems* (co-author F. Casciati). Lucia Faravelli is author or co-author of more than 200 papers on structural reliability, stochastic mechanics, structural control, boundary element analysis and earthquake engineering. She served as Coordinator of the Human Capital Mobility Program of the European Union on Stochastic Mechanics and is chairperson of the Fire Safety Engineering Postgraduate School of the University of Pavia.

GALEA, E. R., was born and educated in Australia. In 1980 he graduated from Monash University with a BSc (honours) and in 1985 he received a Ph.D. in Astrophysics from Newcastle (NSW) University. He has worked in fire safety research since 1986 when he joined the University of Greenwich. His work in fire safety engineering includes the modeling of evacuation, people movement, fire/smoke spread, combustion, and fire extinguishment. Professor Galea's work is applied to applications in the built environment, rail and marine environments as well as aviation. Professor Galea is the author of over 100 academic and professional publications concerning fire and related topics. A recent paper he co-authored with colleagues concerning the EXODUS evacuation model won the prestigious Hodgson Prize, awarded by the Royal Aeronautical Society for the best paper on general subjects (1998). His research and consultancy activities have been supported by a range of organizations including the UK CAA. Fire Research

Station, Home Office, Ove Arup and Partners, EU, EPSRC, HNS, Airbus and Boeing. Professor Galea is the founding director of the Fire Safety Engineering Group (FSEG) at the University of Greenwich. FSEG has developed the fire modeling software SMARTFIRE and the EXODUS suite of evacuation models. These software packages are used by fire safety engineers throughout the world. Professor Galea serves on several British Standards Institute committees concerned with fire safety including FSH/24/5, which deals with issues concerned with life safety and evacuation. Professor Galea was also the nominated UK expert in life safety to the ISO committee concerned with fire safety, ISO TC92 and has recently been appointed to the committee dealing with the validation of fire models. In 1999, he was invited to become a member of the Human Behaviour Task Group of the Society of Fire Protection Engineers (USA).

HOLBORN, PAUL, graduated with a first class honors degree in Physics from Southampton University in 1990. Between 1990 and 1994 he worked as a Research Assistant at the Centre for Nonlinear Dynamics at University College London on a collaborative project with the Fire Safety Engineering Department at Edinburgh University applying the techniques of Nonlinear Dynamics to investigate Flashover in Compartment Fires. He also obtained a Ph.D. in the same research area, which was awarded in 1994. Since 1995 he has been employed as a Research Fellow with the Explosions and Fire Research Unit at South Bank University. During this time he has been involved with a number of research projects, developing and applying fire-sprinkler models to investigate hot gas layer—sprinkler interactions and examining the performance of sprinkler fire protection systems in retail and warehouse applications. He is currently working on a collaborative research project with London Fire Brigade using their Real Fire Research Library—a unique database of information relating to real fires—to evaluate the effectiveness of fire engineering design methodologies and solutions in structures and to assess the abilities of current fire models to predict real fires. His research interests include zone and CFD fire models, sprinkler-hot gas layer interactions, fire protection systems, and fire investigation.

JIA, FUCHEN, has worked in fire field modeling since 1994 when he joined the Fire Safety Engineering Group (FSEG) at the University of Greenwich. Prior to joining FSEG, he obtained an MSc degree from Beijing Institute of Technology in 1987. In October 1999 he successfully defended his Ph.D. thesis. Since 1994 he has published 13 papers with his co-workers in the area of fire field modeling and combustion modeling. Dr. Jia is now a Postdoctoral Research Fellow within FSEG at the University of Greenwich. Dr. Jia's research interest includes CFD, turbulent modeling, gas phase and solid phase combustion models, toxic gas generation and transportation, and radiation models. He is currently involved in extending the combustion and radiation modeling capabilities of the SMARTFIRE fire field model produced by FSEG.

KERAMIDA, ELEFTHERIA P., is a research engineer in the Chemical Engineering Department at the National Technical University of Athens (NTUA). She is studying thermal radiation attenuation phenomena in fires, as a member of the Fire Safety Working Group in NTUA. She holds a Diploma (1995) and a Ph.D. (2000) from NTUA, both in chemical engineering. Email: ellik@chemeng.ntua.gr.

MARKATOS, NIKOLAOS, Diploma Chemical Engineering at the National Technical University of Athens in 1967. M.A. in Business Administration at the Athens School of Economics in 1969. Diploma Imperial College, University of London 1973, Ph.D. in Engineering, Imperial College, University of London in 1974. Process manager in Procter & Gamble Hellas Industry in Athens, 1969-70. Research fellow at Imperial College London, 1973-75. Group leader CHAM Ltd, London 1975-78. Technical Manager 1978-82. Reader at University of Greenwich, London 1982-1986. Director of Section of Mathematical Modeling and Process Analysis, University of Greenwich, London, 1982-86. Professor of National Technical University of Athens since 1985. Director Computational Fluid Dynamics Unit, 1986. Head of Chemical Engineering Department, 1990-94. Rector of National Technical University of Athens, 1991-1997. His scientific interests include transport phenomena in single- and multi-phase flows, computations of turbulence and their engineering and environmental applications. Email: n.markatos@ntua.gr.

MORRIS, I. R., is at the City University, School of Engineering, Northhampton Square London, EC1V 0HB.

PATEL, M. K., is a Reader in Computational Fluid Dynamics at the University of Greenwich and is a senior associate of the Fire Safety Engineering Group (FSEG). He has experience with a number of commercial fluid flow codes including PHOENICS, CFX, Fluent and Smartfire. His interests also lie in the modeling of processes that involve phenomena such as heat and mass transfer, combustion, radiation, turbulence, and multi-phase flow, in both Eulerian and Lagrangian modes. Example of fire-related work includes numerical schemes in fire applications, flow through vents, room fires, adaptive grids, free and forced ventilation, modeling of smouldering fires under micro-gravity conditions, water mist interaction with fire environments in aerospace and marine applications and solid fuel combustion modeling. He is currently involved with the SMARTFIRE development group. Other non-fire modeling related activities include research into the development of User-Interfaces and flow visualization. In the latter area, Dr. Patel has been involved with the development of the FLOWVIS visualization package, which is designed for use in computational fluid dynamics applications. Dr. Patel has published over 60 publications relating to CFD.

TAYLOR, I. R., is a lecturer in Mathematical Modelling in the Faculty of Informatics at the University of Ulster. His research area is concerned with the evaluation of buildings with respect to fire safety or use by disabled people. Much of this involves the integration of computer models with appropriate knowledge bases. In teaching he is particularly interested in the effect of software tools in mathematics on learning and assessment in the curriculum.

SOURIS, NIKOLAOS E., is a Ph.D. candidate in the Chemical Engineering Department at the National Technical University of Athens (NTUA). He is studying water particle heat and mass transfer phenomena. He holds a Diploma (1994) from NTUA in chemical engineering. Email: nsour@chemeng.ntua.gr.

SULLIVAN, PATRICK J. E., is a chartered civil and structural engineer and is the Principal of Sullivan & Associates, consultants in Material & Structural Investigations and Forensic Engineering since 1974. Dr. Sullivan has been a Visiting Professor and Senior Research Fellow, City University, London since 1991. Prior to this date, he was on the teaching and research staff in Concrete Technology at Imperial College of Science and Technology. He was a Specialist Quality Assessor for Higher Education Funding Council for England between 1996-98. He is currently a member/fellow of the Chamber of Architects and Civil Engineers (A & C. E.), the Institute of Civil Engineers, Institution of Structural Engineers, the Societe des Ingenieurs et Scientifique de France, the Chartered Institute of Arbitrators London and the American Concrete Institute. He is also a member on a number of technical committees in the U.K., Europe, and the United States. Before starting his academic and research career, he was employed with Structural and Civil Engineering Consultants and Contractors over a period of ten years and was involved in design of multi-storey structures, shell structures, and in the development, design, and construction of spherical prestressed concrete nuclear pressure vessels. He has been involved in research since 1966 on concrete at fire temperatures, under cryogenic conditions and under other extreme conditions. He has also researched on the effects of bacteria on concrete, the use of organic fibres (juncos) in concrete, the use of waste products (phosphogypsum) on concrete and the effects of low VOC content coatings on Structural steels. Dr. Sullivan has over 70 publications in learned journals and at International Conferences and has innumerable confidential reports for the construction industry and Government Establishments.

TERRO, MOHAMAD JAMIL, is currently Associate Professor of Civil Engineering at the College of Engineering and Petroleum, Kuwait University, Kuwait. His areas of interest include: behavior of concrete and steel structures under fire conditions, durability of concrete and damage assessment and rehabilitation of infrastructure. Dr. Terro was engaged in damage assessment of concrete structures resulting from the civil war in Lebanon and worked as a consultant for the Fire Research Station at the Building Research Establishment in London, U.K. There, his work included reviewing and assessing available numerical models for thermal and structural analysis under fire conditions, and alternative design methods including those suggested in building codes.

ABOUT THE EDITOR

Paul R. DeCicco is Professor Emeritus at the Polytechnic University (New York) where he taught courses in Civil and Fire Protection Engineering and has served as Director of the Center for Fire Research. As principal Investigator in a wide range of fire research projects he has directed full scale fire tests for the New York Fire and Building Departments in connection with the development of building and fire codes. He has also been engaged in mathematical and physical modeling of fire phenomena in various building occupancies, and in the study of fires in large spaces. He is a fellow of the American Society of Civil Engineers and the Society of Fire Protection Engineers and currently serves as Executive Editor of the *Journal of Applied Fire Science.* Professor DeCicco is a registered Professional Engineer and has practiced Civil and Fire Protection Engineering for over forty years. He is co-author of *Making Buildings Safer for People* (Van Nostrand, 1990), and has published a number of papers on fire protection engineering. He has been honored for his research work in fire protection of high-rise buildings and in the improvement of fire safety in high risk urban residential buildings. He is currently engaged as a consultant in the investigation of fires and occasionally serves as an expert witness in fire litigations.

Index